Robben Ford's
URBAN**BLUES**
GUITAR**REVOLUTION**

A Modern Approach to Playing Blues Rhythm Guitar & Dynamic Soloing

ROBBEN **FORD**

TRUEFIRE

Robben Ford's Urban Blues Guitar Revolution

A Modern Approach to Playing Blues Rhythm Guitar & Dynamic Soloing

ISBN: 978-1-78933-234-6

Published by **www.fundamental-changes.com**

www.fundamental-changes.com

Contents

About the Author

Robben Ford is one of the world's most respected electric guitar players, particularly known for his blues playing, as well as his comfort in a variety of musical contexts. A five-time Grammy nominee, he has played with artists as diverse as Joni Mitchell, Jimmy Witherspoon, Miles Davis, George Harrison, Phil Lesh, Bonnie Raitt, Michael McDonald, Bob Dylan, John Mayall, Greg Allman, John Scofield, Susan Tedeschi, Keb Mo, Larry Carlton, Mavis Staples, Brad Paisley, and many more.

A long-time Californian, Robben relocated to Nashville in 2018 in search of new musical inspiration. An avid songwriter with an inclination towards production, he spends much of his time in the studio working on a variety of projects. This new era of creative output features him at the helm, highlighting both up-and-coming artists and some of the best instrumentalists that Music City has to offer.

An essential component of Robben's career has been his commitment to teaching and passing on what he's learnt over the past 40 years to current and future musicians. His instructional videos and clinics over this time have culminated in a collaboration with TrueFire and the birth of the Robben Ford Guitar Dojo. The wealth of his expertise and creativity is generously presented in these state-of-the-art productions and this new book.

Get the Video

Enhance your learning experience!

Thank you for buying this book. To take your learning experience to the next level, we are delighted to be able to offer readers discounted access to the video course on which it is based.

Robben Ford Urban Blues Revolution the video course, features 32 multi-angle one-on-one video lessons with Robben. Get inside Robben's blues language as he breaks down his rhythm and soloing ideas in detail. Close-ups of the fretting and picking hands mean that you'll quickly nail all the essential techniques. Every blues concept is covered here, from scale choices to expressive bends, double-stops, comping and more.

For the complete learning experience, head over to **https://truefire.com/fundamental** and use the code: URBANBLUESBOOK to sign-up for a free account, or scan the QR code below:

Once your account is created, we'll send you a code to purchase the video course at a special price, only available to those who have bought the book.

Introduction

Welcome to my new book, *Urban Blues Guitar Revolution.*

The blues came out of the Southern states of the USA in the late 19th Century and was originally played on acoustic instruments. As it migrated into the cities, each place gradually added its own cultural infusion and this "urbanization" of the blues brought many changes to the style. The most radical change was the electrification of the music. The use of amplifiers and electric guitars gave rise to a variety of new voices in the genre and players began to develop their own signature tones.

In this book, I want to walk you through six complete tunes that highlight this modernization of the blues. First, we'll study the rhythm part of each tune and I'll show you a regular way to play it. Then I'll show you a range of modern comping parts that highlight a more contemporary way of approaching it.

After the rhythm parts, I'll teach you a modern, urban blues solo over the changes. Here you'll be able to learn lots of my blues vocabulary, understand how I think over a tune, and bring your blues playing up to date.

Here's a quick overview of the tunes we're going to cover:

Blues Boogaloo: This tune is inspired by Slim Harpo, master of the Swamp Blues style – a type of blues developed in Baton Rouge, Louisiana, in the 1950s–60s which has a Cajun influence.

Dance Hall Slim: Another Slim Harpo inspired tune, this one has a feel that highlights the Afro-Cuban influence of the Louisiana blues.

Back Street Vamp: I wrote this tune specially for this book, so that you would have the opportunity to learn a more complex blues that has more than the usual three chords. It's a cool, sophisticated urban blues.

King Snake: *King Snake* is a back-to-basics, four-on-the-floor straight up 12-bar! The type of driving blues feel that is often associated with the Texas blues.

Roll With It: Often, at jam sessions, you'll need to solo over a one-chord vamp. In this tune I show you some creative approaches to make things more interesting and build momentum over just one chord.

Sam's Jam: *Sam's Jam* is a different kind of blues that has a surf beat. It's a tribute to Magic Sam, the great Chicago bluesman, and will give you a chance to explore the funkier side of the blues.

* * *

Throughout the book, all the rhythms are clearly notated and include tablature, plus there is free audio to download of every example. There is also a backing track for each tune, so you can jam along with the bass and drums and really lock in the groove.

Each solo has a section-by-section breakdown, where I explain the ideas I've used, and help you to get inside my head and learn where each lick comes from. Use the backing tracks to practice your licks.

Over the course of these tunes, you'll build an understanding of both traditional and modern blues approaches, and learn plenty of cool vocabulary along the way.

Ready? Grab your guitar and let's go!

Robben

Get the Audio

The audio files for this book are available to download for free from **www.fundamental-changes.com.** The link is in the top right-hand corner. Click on the "Guitar" link then simply select this book title from the drop-down menu and follow the instructions to get the audio.

We recommend that you download the files directly to your computer, not to your tablet, and extract them there before adding them to your media library. You can then put them onto your tablet, iPod or burn them to CD. On the download page there are instructions and we also provide technical support via the contact form.

Kindle / eReaders

To get the most out of this book, remember that you can **double tap any image to enlarge it**. Turn off "column viewing" and hold your Kindle in landscape mode.

For over 350 free guitar lessons with videos check out:

www.fundamental-changes.com

Join our free Facebook Community of Cool Musicians

www.facebook.com/groups/fundamentalguitar

Tag us for a share on Instagram: **FundamentalChanges**

Chapter One – Blues Boogaloo Rhythm Parts

Blues Boogaloo was inspired by the music of Louisiana *Swamp Blues* man, Slim Harpo. It has a lilting feel that conjures up the influences of New Orleans blues and Cajun music. Often the rhythm parts for this brand of blues are quite sparse, but what is played is always highly effective. We are going to examine a traditional-type rhythm part for the tune, then we'll expand on this to create a more modern approach.

I'm going to play six variations of this 12-bar blues and, for each one, I'll highlight any sections that need special attention.

The first take features a riff-based idea around a standard A7 barre chord that drops on beat 2 of the bar. What really makes this groove work is the use of a hammer-on from the minor 3rd to the major 3rd on the G string.

To play this, hold down the chord at the fifth fret as if it was an Am7, then hammer on to the 6th fret with your second finger. I've shown this idea in the diagram below. Play the barre chord with all the black notes, then hammer onto the hollow note.

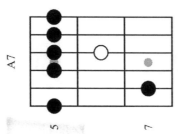

Each bar of A7 is based around this hammer-on idea, but the rhythm and strumming patterns vary slightly each time. Throughout this book, I want you to listen carefully to the accompanying audio tracks, so that you can copy my rhythmic variations. Often this is easier than reading the notation, and once you get the idea you can adlib your own variations. The blues is organic, roots music, and these small variations are what brings the music to life.

First, a word about my strumming technique.

When I play a rhythm part like this, I keep my strumming hand loose, relaxed, and continuously moving up and down, whether it's connecting with the strings or not. The strumming hand should act like a metronome, keeping the time solid. When I do connect with the strings, most often I'll be playing a downstroke.

Let's get used to the basic strumming pattern on which all the rhythmic variations are based.

The *groove* is all in the fretting hand. When you see an "X" in the notation/tab, you'll lift your fretting hand very slightly – just enough to mute the strings. As you hit the strings, it should make a percussive snap but not sound any notes.

The strumming hand's continuous movement is the *engine room* of this rhythm part, and the fretted chord accents *pop out* to create the groove. Getting both hands coordinated is crucial to capturing the feel.

First, play through this rhythm exercise with all strings muted. Listen to the audio, take things slowly, and make sure you're placing the accented strokes in the right place (indicated by > in the notation).

Rhythm Exercise 1

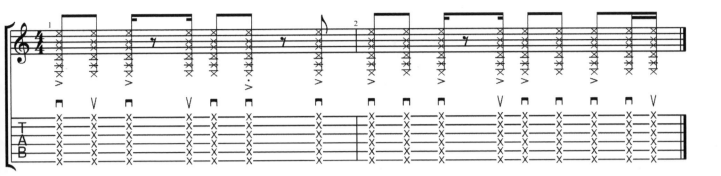

Once you are confident that you've nailed the rhythm and you can hear the accents popping out, it's time to play it with the A7 chord. This will take a little more concentration as you add in the hammer-on, but it's the exact same rhythm. Learn it slow and program it into muscle memory.

Rhythm Exercise 2

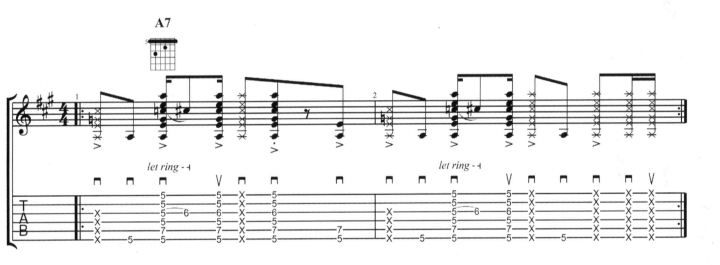

We'll return to this groove shortly, but first we move on to the opening bars of *Blues Boogaloo*. This blues is in the key of A Major and the introduction begins on the V chord (E). We then move to an F#5 chord and walk up in half steps until we land on the A root.

The chord shapes might look a little unusual in the notation, but I'm just holding a barre chord from the fifth string. I'll often fret barre chords this way – played with my thumb hooked over the neck – because they are easier to play than a full barre and they help give these chords the attack they need to punch through a band mix.

Notice too, that I avoid playing the major 3rd interval on the G string by muting it with my second finger. This makes the chords sound a little more aggressive, and it serves to highlight the color of the 3rd when the verse kicks in.

Example 1a

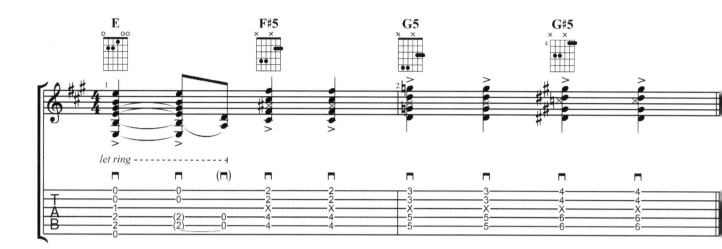

After the introduction, we begin the first 12-bar take on *Boogaloo Blues*. The first four bars use the A7 riff you just learnt but watch out for the small rhythmic variations.

When the progression moves to the IV chord (D), I'm using a first inversion D7, so that the chord can be arranged on the top four strings. D7 has the notes D (root), F# (3rd), A (5th) and C (b7). This voicing has the 3rd as the lowest note and is often written as D/F# on chord charts. Importantly, I wanted the A note on top, so that it keeps that note in common with the A7 chord.

Here's how to play it:

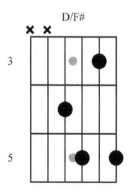

The rhythm in bars 5-6 can be tricky at first, so listen carefully to the audio example to hear how I play it.

In bar five, the first two 1/8th notes are muted accents. The chord sounds on beat 2 and is a dotted 1/8th note, which means it's held for the duration of one 1/8th note plus half as much again, before the next chord accent sounds.

In bar six, the first 1/8th note is muted, followed by two quick 1/16th note chord accents. Written down, it looks more difficult than it is. The muted accents fall exactly on beats 1 and 2, so you just need to get a quick double strum in before playing the accent on beat 2.

Example 1b

The E7 chord that begins the final four-bar section is also a first inversion voicing, with G# as the lowest note. It's the same shape you used for the D7 chord, shifted up two frets. Bar twelve ends with a trademark blues passing riff that will become a feature of the next take.

Example 1c

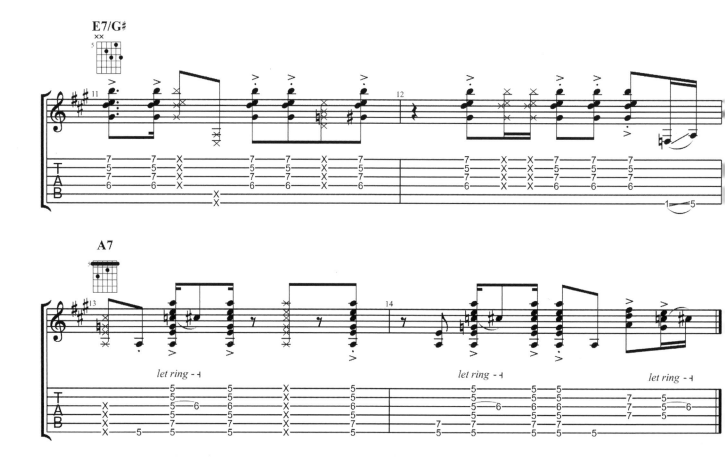

For the second take of this tune, I've included a pickup bar in the notation, as the riff that ended the previous example crosses the bar line.

In bar four, I introduce a new chordal idea for the IV chord. I'm only holding down partial voicings, but the sound created is the movement from E9 to D9. Neither chord is played with a root note. Play this chord movement more slowly and you might recognize the main riff from the Miles Davis tune *Freddie Freeloader*.

Example 1d

The next eight-bar section of this take has similar rhythmic variations but notice the "late" D7 chord in bar ten. Instead of playing a whole bar of D7, here it is used as a passing chord.

Example 1e

The third 12-bar variation introduces a more modern approach and draws on ideas from funk and RnB. First, the strumming rhythm places some chord accents on the beat and some on the offbeat. The effect of this is that certain accents sound *pushed* i.e. they anticipate the beat. This gives the rhythm a real sense of momentum.

Second, the chords in this take include some voicings more common to jazz than blues, and they are mostly arranged on the bottom four strings. The diagrams below show how to play the chord shapes you've not already encountered.

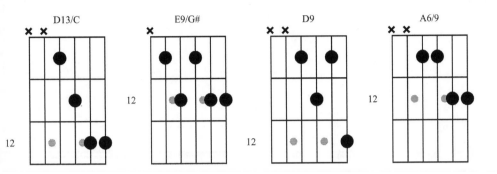

Here is take three in full.

Example 1f

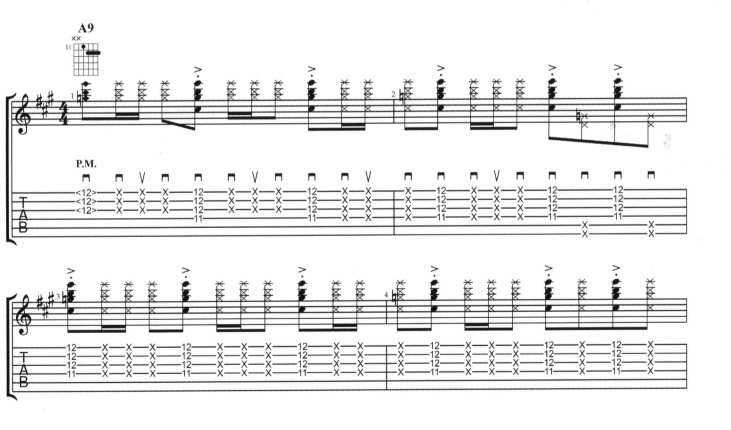

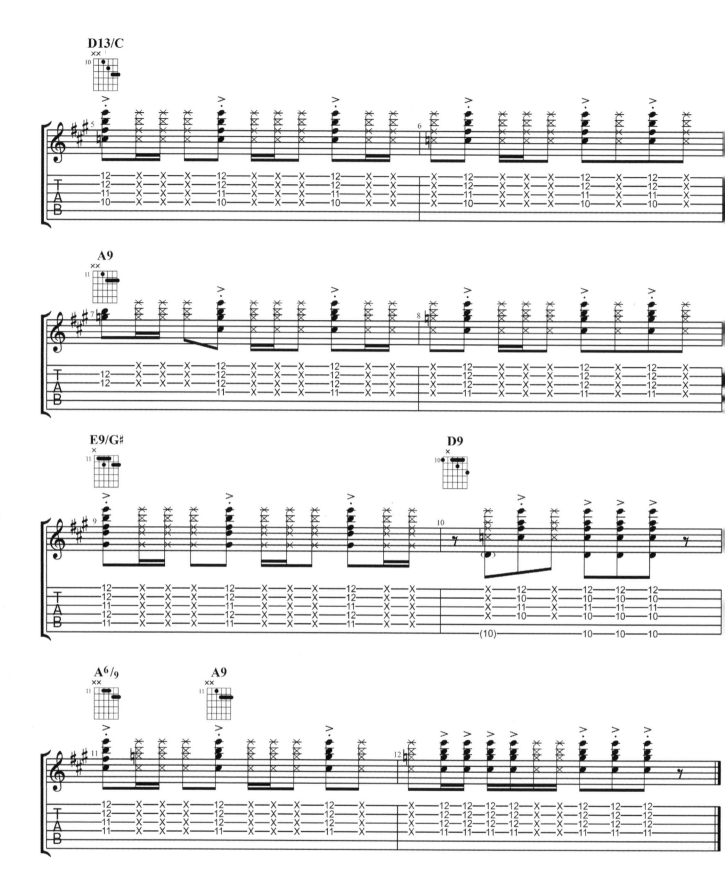

The next pass of the tune features an RnB style riff that moves from a minor chord to a dominant chord. The riff is a looping four-bar phrase that begins with muted 1/8th note accents and has the first chord accent on beat 2.

We are using fragments of Em and D chords to approach the A7. This movement is then reversed to get back to the Em. The E minor chord does not belong to the key of A Major, so you may be wondering where this idea comes from. It's common in jazz to play a minor chord or arpeggio built from the 5th degree of a dominant chord. A7 has the notes A, C#, E (5th), G, so we can superimpose E minor ideas over it to produce a different color. Listen to the audio, then play through the riff.

Example 1g

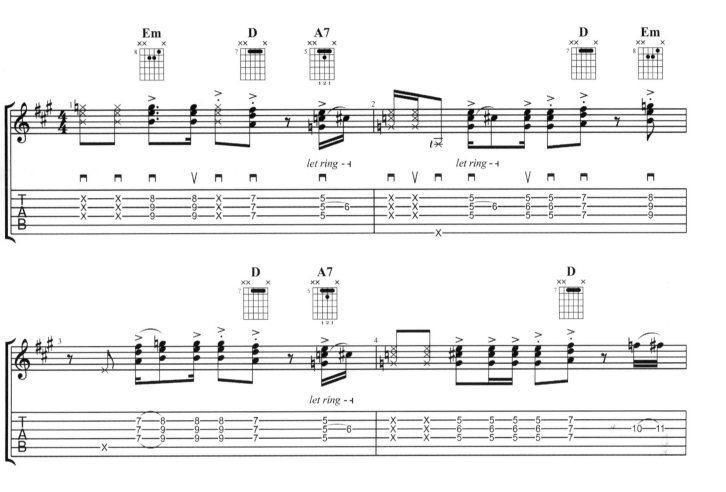

When the progression changes to the IV chord, we can simply slide the riff up the neck to be based around the D7 chord at the tenth fret. Here is the rest of the take from bar five onwards. I like to incorporate open strings wherever possible, so notice the full voicing of E7 in the final bar. Adding the open strings creates a more powerful sound.

Example 1h

Here's a simple but effective idea you can use to create interest in a blues. This take adds sus4 and sus2 chord voicings to add some tension and release to the music. A Major is a great key to use for this idea as we can take advantage of the open strings to produce a classic jangly chord sound. It changes the whole timbre of the rhythm part and moves away from the tight, riff-based sound to a more open sound.

Here are the suspended chord shapes. The A7sus4 is a rootless shape. This D7sus2 is a great open voicing with the suspended 2nd (E) on top.

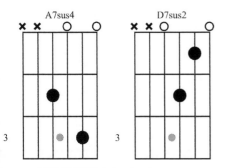

Now, here is the full 12-bar chorus:

Example 1i

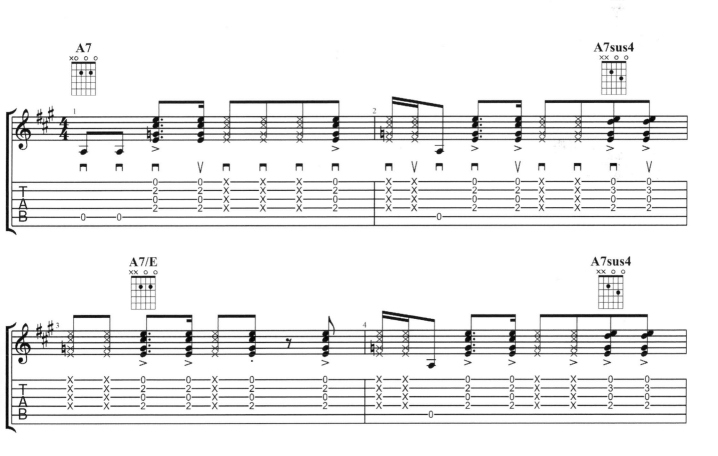

The next chorus takes the classic 12-bar riff we all learnt when we first began playing blues and adapts it for the boogaloo feel. It doesn't need much explanation, other than to say instead of playing the expected repetitive version, we are breaking up the rhythm to make things less predictable and more riff-like. Try it out!

Example 1j

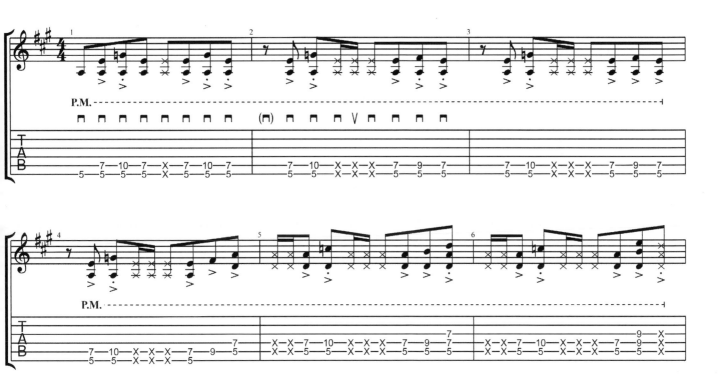

For contrast, the final 12-bar section returns to a funkier feel, but this time with more colorful chord voicings. These chords have extended or altered notes and are more commonly found in jazz. Played over the three-chord blues sequence, however, with a hard-hitting funk feel, they bring a unique flavor to the music. Let's take a look at the chords.

Let's think about the ways in which we can spice up a basic A7 chord.

First, we can add extended notes i.e. other notes from the parent scale of the chord.

We are in the key of A Major, which has the notes: A, B, C#, D, E, F#, G#

The A7 chord is built from the notes A (root), C# (3rd), E (5th) and G (b7). The A13/G shape below omits the root and adds B and F# notes, which are the 9th and 13th degrees of the scale respectively. This idea is repeated for the D13 chord.

Second, we can use altered notes i.e. scale notes that have been flattened or sharpened. I'll spare you any heavy theory here, but there are only four ways in which a dominant chord can be altered: the fifth and ninth degrees of the scale can be flattened or sharpened to give us four altered notes to play with.

Below, a simple three-note A7 chord has two notes added: C and F (on the B and high E strings respectively). The C note is the #9 and the F is the #5 degree of the scale. The resulting chord is usually written A7(#5#9). Sometimes on lead sheets you'll just see A7alt written, which means it's an altered dominant chord, but you get to choose which of the four possible altered notes to add.

The final new chord is a voicing of E9 that has the root note on the high E string and the 3rd (G#) as the lowest note.

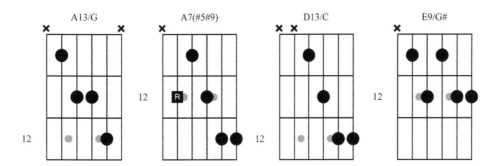

This example has more of a 1/16th note feel than previous versions, and the groove is created by controlling which chord accents are muted and which are allowed to pop out. Remember that your strumming arm is the metronome and now you need to crank up the speed to play constant 1/16th note, up-down strums.

Example 1k

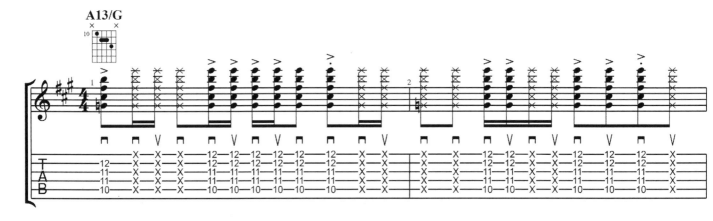

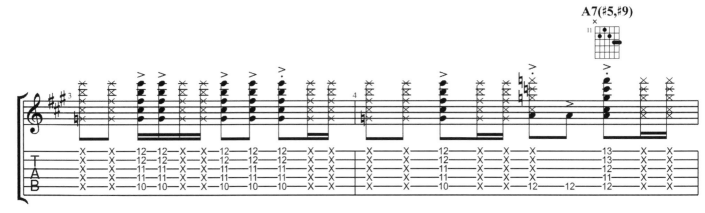

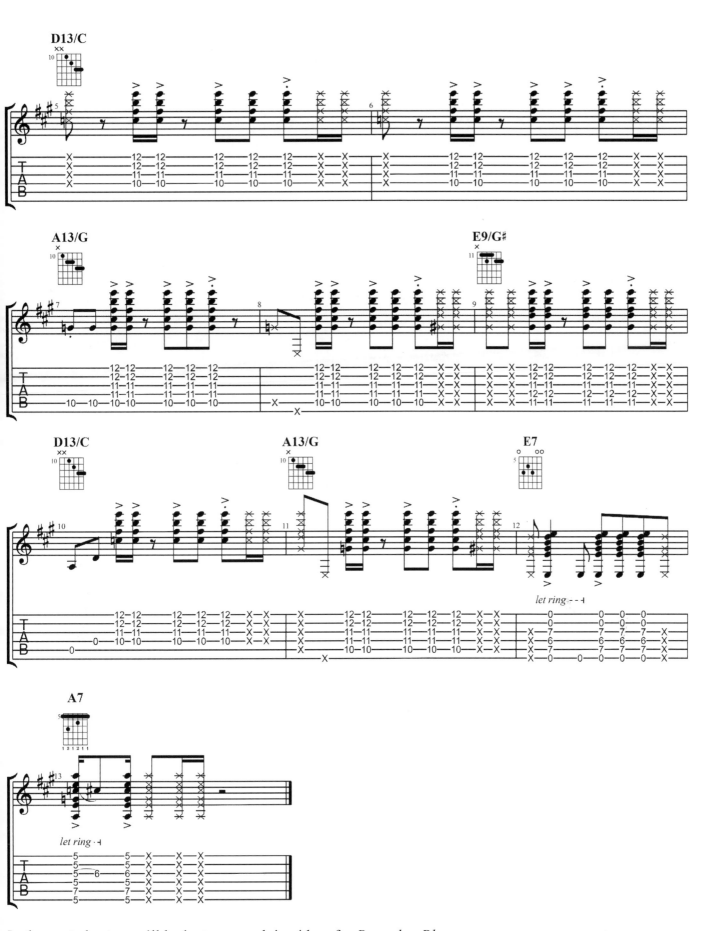

In the next chapter we'll look at some soloing ideas for *Boogaloo Blues*.

Chapter Two – Boogaloo Blues Soloing Approach

Now you're familiar with the feel and vibe of *Boogaloo Blues*, I want to show you some different approaches to soloing over it. Below are three solo takes, each of which features a central idea from which the melodic phrases stem. We'll examine each solo in turn and I'll highlight break down for you what I'm playing.

This first example begins by outlining the chromatic ascending chords played in the introduction. The root note of each chord is located on the high E string, and the notes on the G string are a sixth below each root. Playing phrases in 6ths is a big part of Country and Blues music.

As the solo begins in bar three, notice that throughout I play complete phrases that have a beginning, a middle and an end. It's very easy and tempting to just noodle over the blues, but playing complete musical statements, leaving a breath between each one, tells a story and gives your solo purpose and direction.

At the end of bar six comes the central idea of this solo: playing phrases containing triplets. Over a driving groove like *Boogaloo Blues,* playing triplets has the effect of pulling against the beat. Listen to the audio recording and you'll hear that I also play these phrases slightly behind the beat, which heightens the effect. There are times where you'll want to play slightly in front of the beat to create a sense of urgency, but here playing just behind creates a cool, unhurried vibe.

To learn the solo, work on each complete phrase, rather than a bar at a time. Try to memorize each phrase and when you find something you really like, move it other areas of the neck or transpose it to other keys.

Example 2a

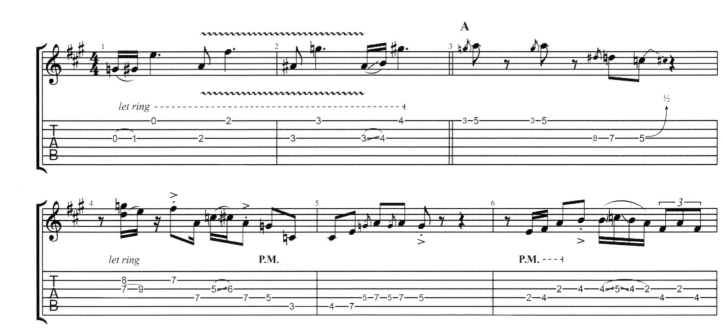

An important part of the language of blues guitar is developing motifs. A motif is just a simple musical phrase that is stated, then repeated and developed. When the idea is developed, it might use the same notes, or different notes with a similar rhythm.

Another important idea in blues is the *question and answer* phrase. Similar to a motif, a musical statement is made (the question) and the answer comes with a different phrase, which can be followed by another question, and so on. This taps into the idea that originally the blues was sung unaccompanied, and was also sung in groups, often with one person singing a line and the rest "answering" it. Transferring this idea onto guitar is a great way to achieve vocal-like phrasing.

Both of these ideas are used in the first four bars of the second solo. You'll clearly hear the motif of bar one repeated in bar three. Take all four bars together and we have a *question, answer, question, answer* format. If you are ever struggling for ideas to play, a great place to begin is to come up with just one strong phrase. Then you can repeat it and adapt it. In bar three, you can hear that I've taken the phrase of bar one and developed it by adding an additional bend. This, in turn, led to the idea played in bar four.

Example 2b

Lastly, here is a quite different approach. The first half of this take is a chord solo. The backing band are sticking to the basic three-chord changes, which means we can take some liberties with the chords we play over the top and it won't clash with the backing. On the audio track it might sound like I'm playing *outside* at times, but in fact all I'm doing is using more colorful dominant chord voicings that contain extended and altered notes. To bring some contrast to this outside-inside section, I bring the solo home with more traditional sounding blues licks.

Let's take a look at those altered chords. We've already encountered 13th, suspended chords and 6/9 chord voicings. The two new voicings used in bar four are the ones that are causing the brief tension in the music. Here's how to play them:

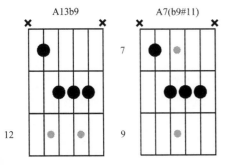

A13b9 is an altered dominant chord with an added extension. Remember, our frame of reference for this chord is A7. This voicing adds the 13th (F#) extended note and flat 9 (Bb) altered note.

Even more tense sounding is the A7b9#11 chord that follows. Notice that it's the exact same shape as A13b9, moved down three frets. If we compare this chord to the original A7, we see that it has no root note and is constructed (low to high) E (5th), Bb (b9), D# (#11) and G (13th). The #11 sound creates a lot of tension that begs to be resolved, and this is useful to create some excitement and drama in a solo.

Take some time to study the rhythmic ideas of the chord solo section. It begins by punching out 1/8th note stabs, but then breaks things up by playing stabs on the offbeat. All the accents are played on the offbeat in bars 5-6, which really makes them stand out.

Example 2c

Chapter Three – Dance Hall Slim Rhythm Parts

The next song we'll look at is a piece called *Dance Hall Slim.* As the name suggests, this is another tune inspired by Slim Harpo, who came from Louisiana, so it has that *Swamp Blues* feel to it. Music like this is intended to be quite repetitive and it has that strong RnB pulse.

This tune is in the key of F and is one of those pieces of music that crops up a lot in the blues. Is it in F Major or F minor? The answer is both! We begin in F Major, but later the song freely moves between the two tonal centers.

First, we'll walk through the basic rhythm pattern for the tune. The more traditional rhythm part we're going to look at spells out the harmony very simply, using chord voicings with only two or three notes. This minimal chordal approach creates a powerful sound which really serves to establish the groove.

You'll hear that it has a strong emphasis on the "1" and "2&" beats of the bar. It's an unusual rhythm for the blues and creates a heavy, swinging groove that has a lot of attitude. First, let's examine the repeating two-bar rhythm pattern. On the audio you'll hear that I play muted accents between the chords, but first we'll isolate the chord accents which are the heart of the groove.

The rhythm has an 1/8th note triplet feel. Notice that only the first accent (F5) is played on the beat, and the rest fall on off beats. The Ab5 chord is held for a 1/4 note, which helps to create the "floating" feel after the two punchy accents. Listen to the audio to get the idea, then try this out.

Example 3a

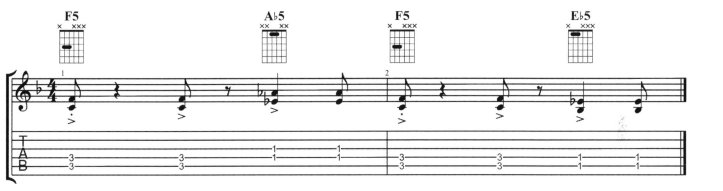

Once you have the above rhythm locked in, you can add the muted accents in between. Place a heavier accent on the chords and play lighter for the muted accents. Those chords really need to jump out of the groove!

Example 3b

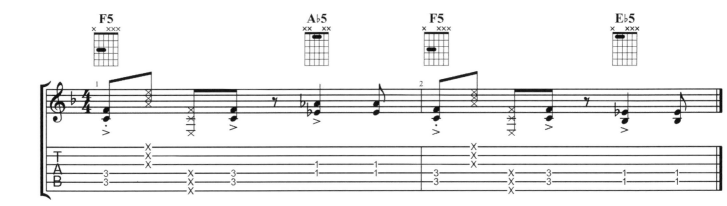

Once you are comfortable with Example 3b, work through the full blues sequence applying the rhythm. Play along to the *Dance Hall Slim* backing track and really focus on getting the groove to sit in the pocket.

Example 3c

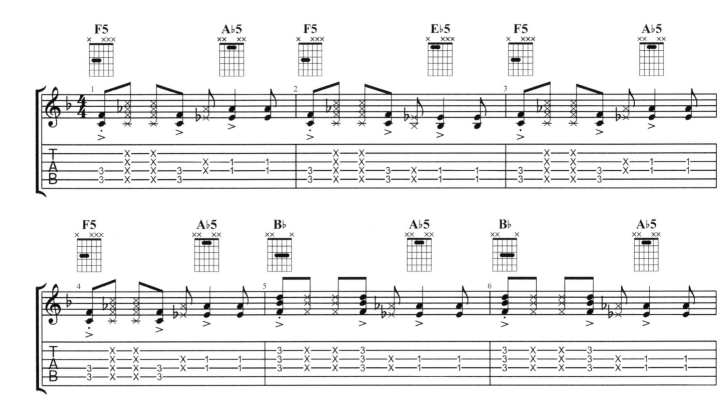

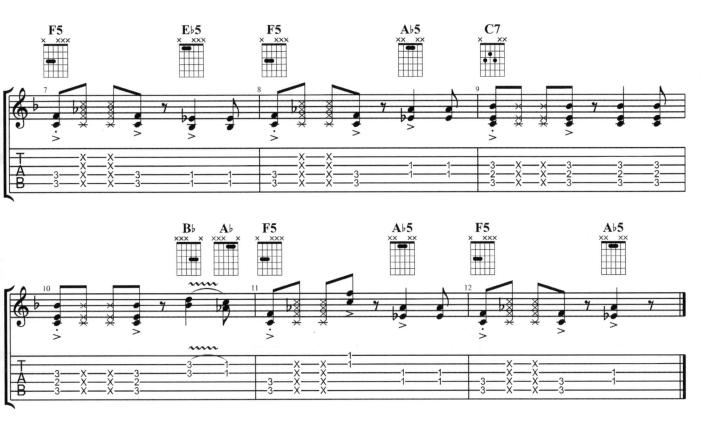

So, what can we do to give a tune like this a more contemporary sound, which in turn will lead to more modern sounding soloing approaches? We can spice up the chords to add more depth to the harmony, and we can also begin to introduce some rhythmic variations. Throughout the following alternative takes we will add different altered dominant and minor chord voicings and make subtle changes to the rhythm.

This second take on the rhythm part begins with an Fm chord inversion that has the b3 (Ab) as the lowest note.

This is followed by a common dominant 7#9 shape (the Hendrix chord) for the F7#9 chord. When the progression reaches the C7 chord in bar nine, we play a rootless C7#9 three-note shape.

If you know your jazz chords, then the Bb9 chord in bar five may look like a Dm7b5 shape to you. It's actually a Bb9 with the Bb root omitted, and the 3rd (D) as the lowest note. It's often written as Bb9/D on chord charts. Here are the chord grids:

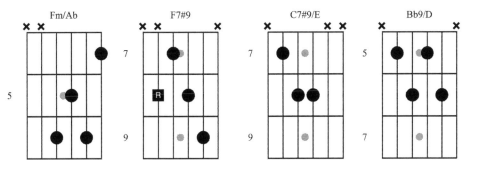

Now listen to the audio for the second take of the rhythm part. Notice that I simplified the rhythm in bars 1-4 to bring some variation, and this serves to really open things up. The rhythm is further broken up in bars 5-12 as we introduce some alternative strumming patterns that begin to move away from the original rhythm part. Play through it now.

Example 3d

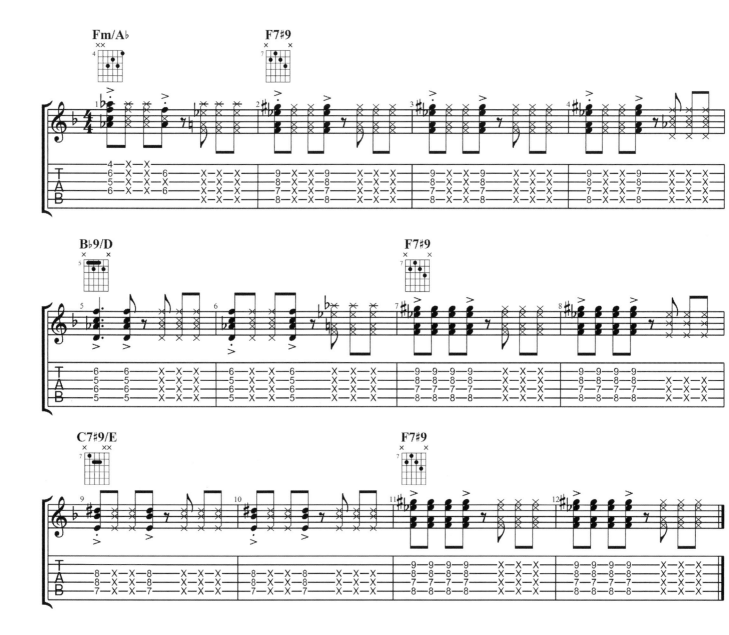

The next version has more of a minor feel and uses several minor chord variations. Often, it's worth experimenting with subtle variations of the chord voicings to enrich the harmony and introduce a point of difference. Again, many of these chords have more in common with jazz harmony, but most are played as quick stabs and they add a fresh sound to the tune. Here are the new chord voicings:

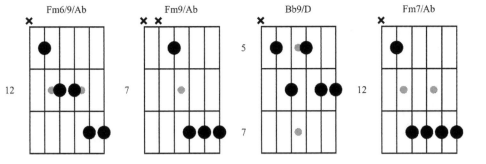

In bar nine, the C7#5#9 chord has no root note and an E (the 3rd) in the bass. This voicing can be tricky to grip if you're not used to it. Play the E note on the A string, fret 7, with the first finger. The second finger will then barre the top four strings at fret 8. Lastly, the pinkie frets the B string at fret 9. Gripping the chord this way should enable you to hear every note clearly.

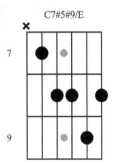

This version of the song, which has a strong minor vibe throughout, ends in bar twelve with an F Major riff. This is a surprise to the ears after what has gone before, and really grabs the listener's attention.

Example 3e

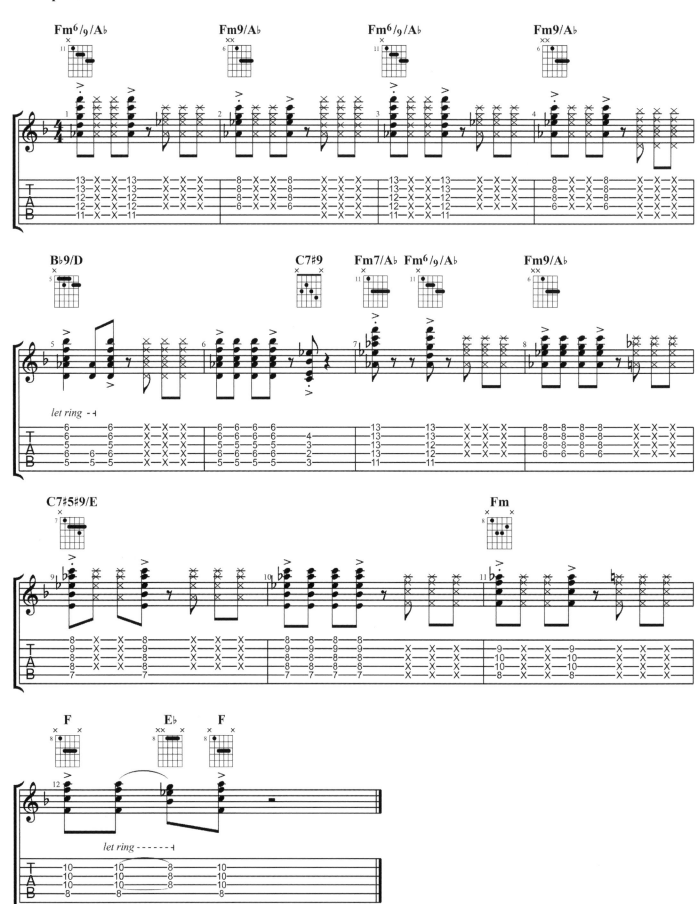

Next, here is a simple rhythmic variation you can apply to this tune. It's a *skank* type rhythm, often used in Reggae, with accents on the offbeat. I'll illustrate it with the first few bars, but you can apply this idea to the whole tune.

Example 3f

Lastly, here is another take on the tune with some different chordal variations. It's another minor feel chorus, but this time using minor 11 chords.

If you're faced with playing several bars of a minor chord, an effective way of keeping things interesting is to shift up a whole step, then back down to the original chord. If you apply a strong rhythmic feel to this idea, you've got a solid sounding riff. In this example, because I chose a high Fm7 voicing, it actually sounds as though I'm shifting *down* to the Gm11. Here is the chord shape:

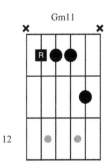

Bar nine features an unusual full voicing of Cm11 as a twist, instead of playing the expect C7 chord. The last two bars use the Fm11 shape below. Here, Bb is the lowest note and the root is located on the high E string.

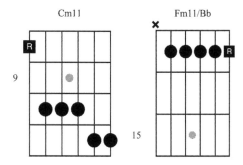

Example 3g

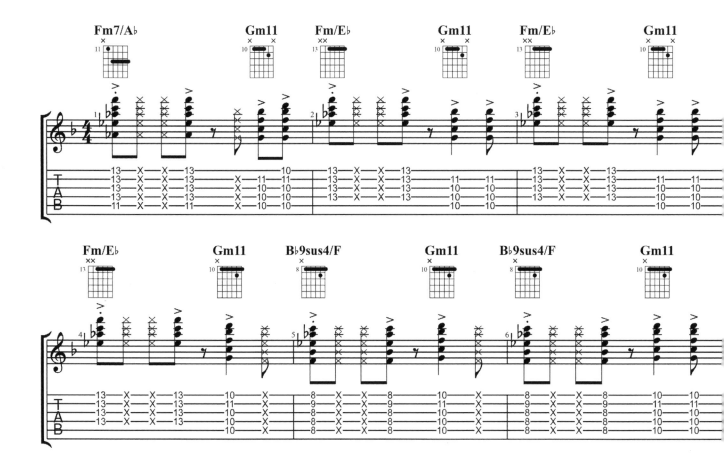

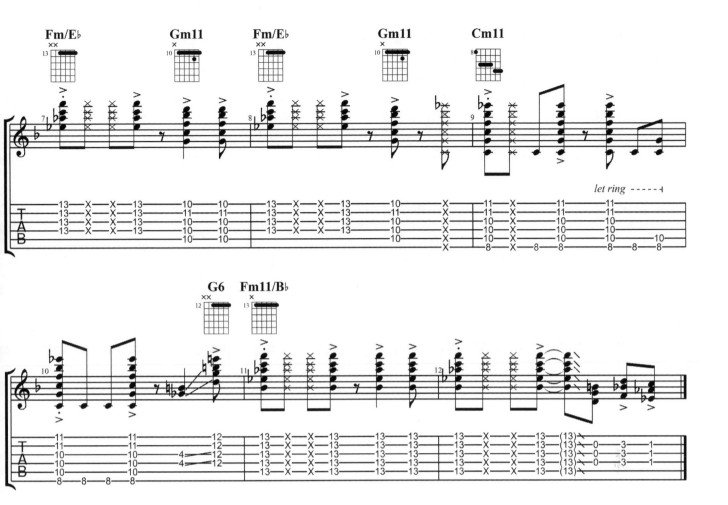

Next, let's look at some ideas for soloing over this tune.

Chapter Four – Dance Hall Slim Soloing Approach

Much of the language of the blues is based around pentatonic scales. When soloing, blues players will freely switch between minor and major pentatonic scale ideas and mix them up to create different moods. Players often write off pentatonic scales as being too simple or boring, but there is so much music in them! What is boring is getting stuck in the same old patterns, but used creatively pentatonic scales are incredible tools. Remember too that the blues is an expressive art form, so using these scales to improvise is about getting the most out of every single note and good phrasing is very important.

I'm a huge fan of saxophone players and among my favorites are Paul Desmond, Wayne Shorter and Sonny Rollins. We can learn a lot about good phrasing from these players and I suggest it would be good to listen to some of their music, rather than just guitar players! Horn players are forced to take a breath when they play, so they tend to play succinct phrases. Guitarists, on the other hand, can be guilty of playing lines that are too long and don't begin/end cleanly. Listen to a player like Sonny Rollins on his famous tune *St Thomas* and you'll hear that he begins his solo with just a couple of notes, and from a simple start develops a theme that just builds and builds.

In this first solo, you'll see that I begin by making short musical statements in a question and answer style and leave lots of breaths. Don't be afraid to leave space in your solo – it makes the notes you *do play* stand out all the more. Try it out now.

Example 4a

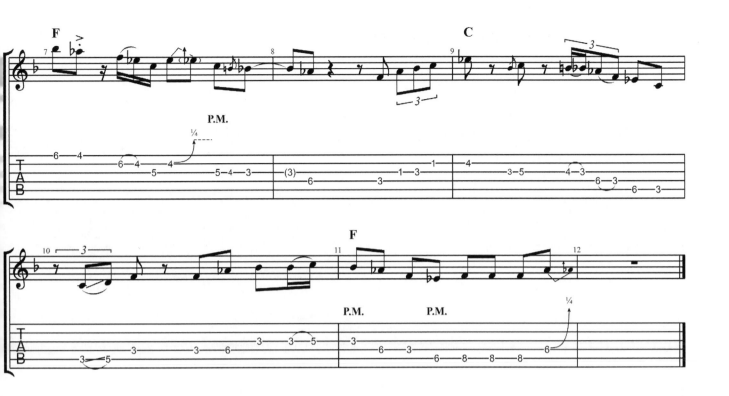

Building on the previous chorus, this solo begins to build in intensity and the phrases are a little more complex. One tip to bear in mind is that if you're going to play fast, complex phrases, it's good to balance them with slower, more expressive ones.

Here are a few things to notice in this solo.

Listen to the audio and you'll hear that I add a lot of vibrato to the first note of bar one. To mimic this, once the note is bent to the correct pitch (a half step), add vibrato by rapidly moving your finger vertically (floor to ceiling). Also loosen your grip on the guitar neck slightly, so that it can move with you. This expressive opening phrase leads into a fast triplet phrase in bar two. Slow this phrase down and get all the notes under your fingers before you bring it up to speed.

In bar four, to lead into the Bb bar, this seven-note phrase spells an Fm6 arpeggio. The inclusion of the 6th gives it a more modern sound. Give the guitar neck a shake to get that vibrato!

The triplet phrase that begins in bar seven crosses into the next bar, so keep an eye on your timing here.

In bar nine there is a small detail worth pointing out. The last note of the bar is a Bb, which is the b7 of the C7 chord. This is approached chromatically from above. Targeting a chord tone and hitting it on the beat is always a strong sound and you can use passing notes (notes that don't belong to the key) to approach it from above or below.

Work through the solo and when you've got it sounding smooth, try it over the backing track.

Example 4b

The final solo takes the intensity up another notch and incorporates a more complex run that occurs in bar four. Let's take a look at this idea.

One thing I like to do in my playing is to create tension by briefly playing "outside" the tonality. It's a great way of bringing the blues up to date and creating a more modern sound. When I do this, I always have a *target* note in mind that will resolve the tension and bring things back inside.

Bar five is the point at which the progression changes to the Bb chord. An easy way to create tension is to anticipate that chord change by approaching it from a half step above. If you play through the blues sequence now, and on the last beat of bar four play a B7 chord just before the Bb7 in bar five, you'll hear this in action and realize it's a very common idea used a lot in the blues.

So, for the whole of bar four, I'm playing in a B tonality, then the line resolves to a Bb note on the first beat of bar five. To make the most of this tension, I'm playing an altered scale that contains a lot of tension notes.

All the notes come from the B Half-Whole Diminished scale. This scale is used more in jazz than blues, but over the years I've incorporated it into my playing and it's become part of my signature sound.

The B Half-Whole Diminished scale contains the notes B, C, D, Eb, F, F#, G# and A.

It's called the *Half-Whole* scale because from the root note it follows a half-step, whole-step, half-step continuous pattern. This is evident when you see it laid out on the fretboard. Notice it has the exact same pattern on every string.

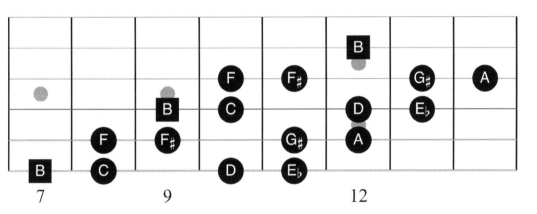

If you've never thought about using an idea like this in the blues, it might seem a bit radical to you – and somewhat dissonant to your ears at first – but give it a try. To practice this, play this scale over any dominant 7th chord from its root note. Over a regular dominant 7 chord, the Half-Whole scale will naturally highlight b9, #9 and #11 tension notes.

To nail the phrase in bar four, I suggest slowing things right down and learning it in four-note blocks before joining them together.

Example 4c

Chapter Five – Back Street Vamp Rhythm Parts

I wrote *Back Street Vamp* especially for this book, so that you'd have the opportunity to learn a more complex, modern blues that has more going on harmonically than the usual three chords. I call this a "vamp" because the entire sequence spans just two bars then rolls around continuously. It doesn't feel like that when you listen to the song, however, because it's played at a very slow tempo. The notation below shows the basic chord changes.

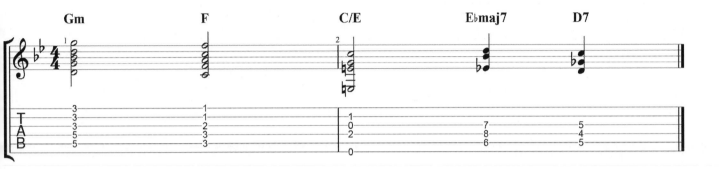

In the next chapter I'll talk more about where these chords come from as we consider how to improvise over them, but in this chapter we're going to look at how you can play variations of these basic changes to keep the rhythm part interesting and engaging.

When playing in a band setting, a great lesson to learn is that we often *don't* need to play full chord voicings to outline the harmony, even when the guitar is the main harmonic instrument. We can play very small structures – fragments of chords, in fact – and still provide our audience with enough information about the harmony of the tune.

Back Street Vamp has a very open, spacious feel and, to begin with at least, we want to preserve that. Here's a way of revealing the harmony with small chord forms, which can be used in a riff-like way.

Example 5a

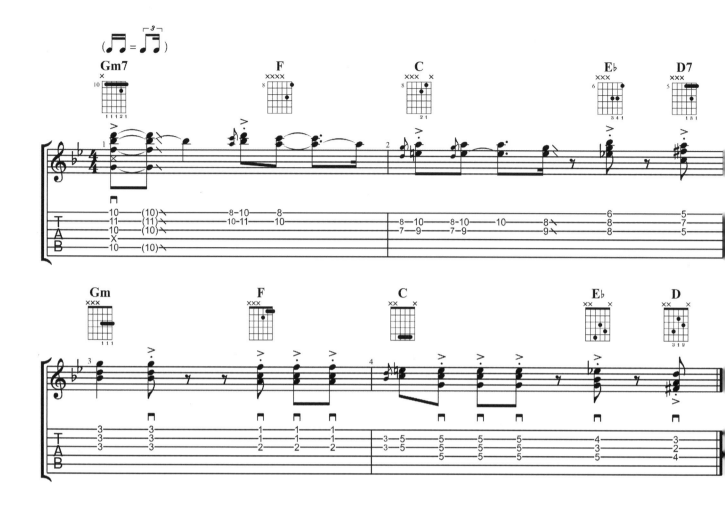

In order to take *Back Street Vamp* into modern blues territory, Example 5b begins to introduce some more colorful chord voicings. In bar one, the chord played in the second half of the bar is a *quartal voicing*, which just means that the chord comprises notes stacked in intervals of a 4th.

Quartal chords are quite ambiguous in nature and can be interpreted in different ways depending on the context. This stack of notes could be viewed as Am11, for instance, but what is happening in the bass gives the chord its context. Played over the bass player's F root note, it creates the sound of F6/9.

In bar two, the Ebmaj9 chord is a rootless shape. The diagram below shows the full version of the chord, with the position of the root indicated by the hollow note.

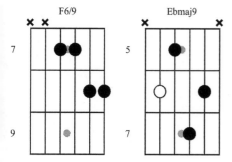

In this take on the rhythm part, notice that I switch between some punchy rhythms and more laid-back palm muted picking. This gives the part some light and shade.

Two more chord voicings to notice here occur at the end of bar four. The Ebmaj7 and D7 chords are both voiced with the 5th in the bass (Bb and A notes respectively). These were chosen to create a descending bassline that will lead to the Gm chord that will follow them.

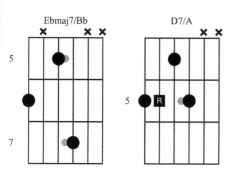

Example 5b

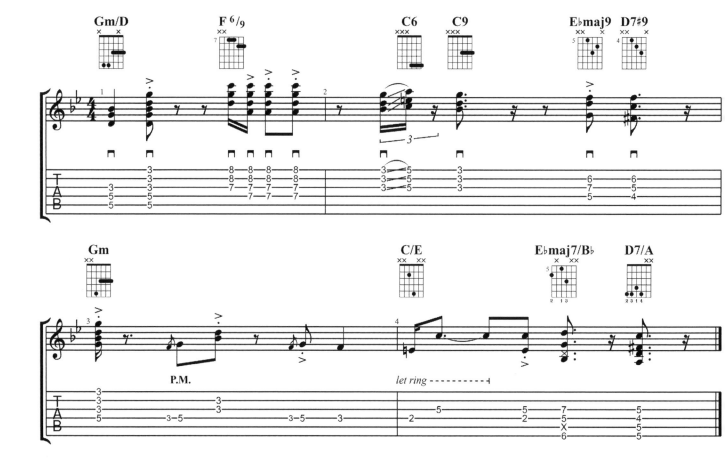

In keeping with the cool, laid-back vibe of this tune, and as a contrast to the chordal passages, a muted picking approach through the changes can be very effective.

Example 5c

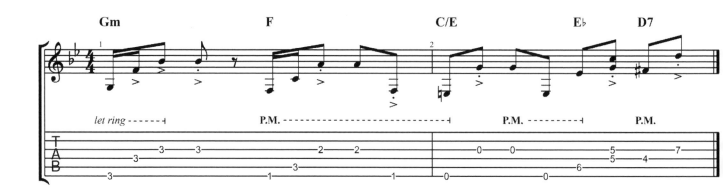

After a passage like this, which brings the focus down, we have the room to go somewhere, so we can return to the chords and play a strong rhythm pattern to anchor down the groove. You've encountered all of these extended or altered chords in previous chapters, so in this example, concentrate on the chord accents and play the part with lots of confidence and attitude!

The only tricky part is the fast chord changes in bar four. You just need to hold down the three chord grids indicated in the notation/tab – for the in-between chords I'm just picking out fragments of them.

Example 5d

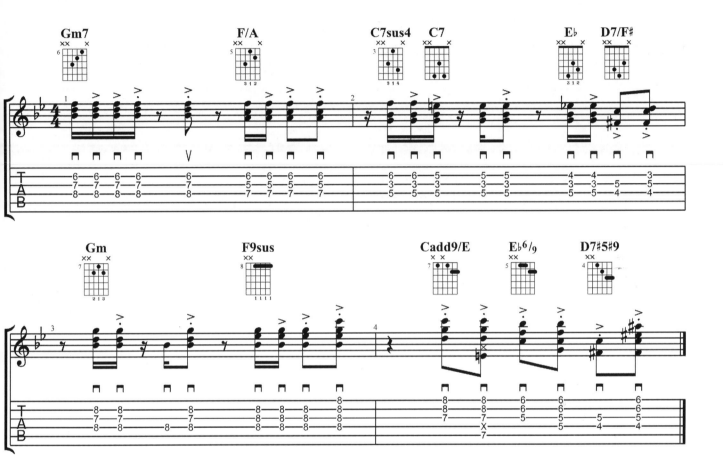

When a chord progression is looping around like this one, in order to keep things interesting we can intersperse full chords with short riff-like phrases or even single note passages. Example 5e takes this approach.

One new chord is introduced in bar six – the Major 13#11. This is a rare major chord that has both extended and altered notes. Here's how to play it:

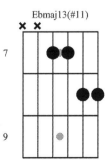

Ebmaj13(#11)

Notice that it's the exact same shape as the C6/9 chord that precedes it. You may remember that you encountered this chord in Example 5a, but there it was called F6/9. How come?

This illustrates the point that context determines the sound of a quartal chord. The bass player's note choice underneath will change its sound and suggest different tonalities – much like a piano player can hold the same chord in the right hand, but create a variety of "new" chords, just by playing different bass notes in the left hand.

With a C note underpinning the above shape, the sound is C6/9. With an F in the bass, it's F6/9. Here, superimposed over an Eb note, it's the sound of Ebmaj13#11, and the notes represent the #11, 7th, 3rd and 13th from low to high. If you like, you can play the full chord voicing by adding the root note on the A string, fret 6.

Example 5e

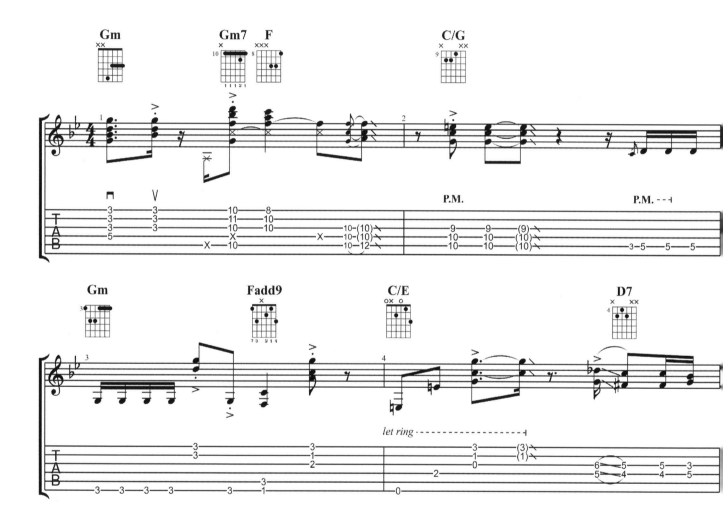

48

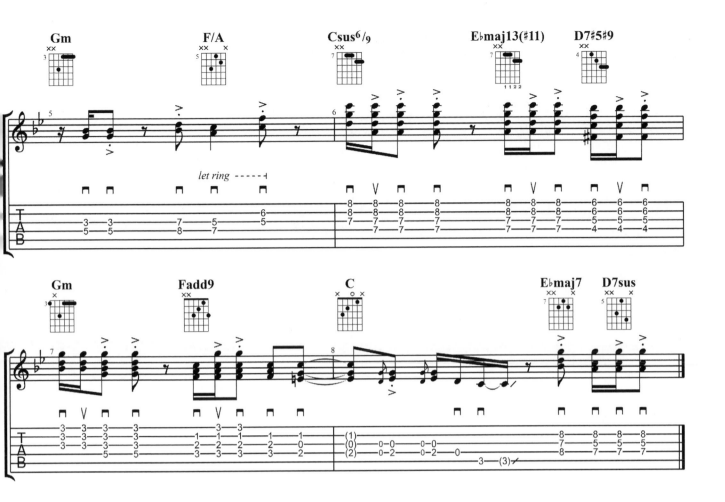

Another approach to rhythm playing I often use is to create a repeating motif that moves through the changes. Blues soloists do this all the time when improvising melodic lines, but we can also express this idea with chords. Each chord change here states a simple phrase played on the high strings.

Example 5f

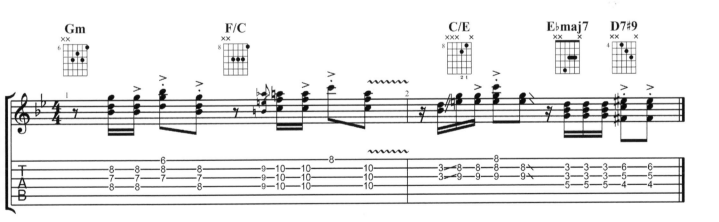

Here's a variation on this idea, but this time the chordal motif is played using only two-note structures.

Example 5g

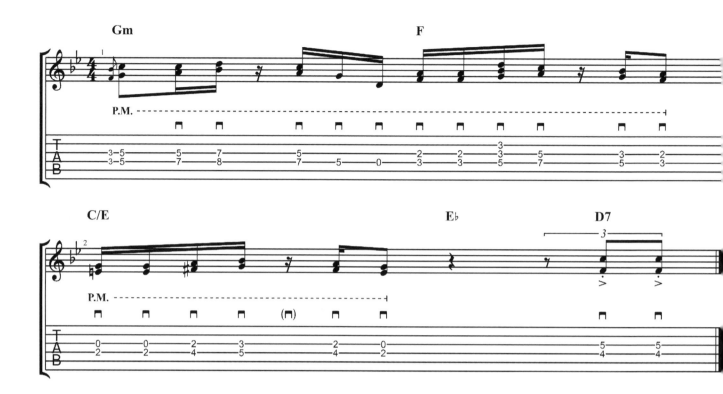

Lastly, here is one more variation on this idea. Playing "chord phrases" like this blurs the lines a little between what constitutes rhythm and lead playing, but they are incredibly useful for making strong, memorable melodic statements.

Example 5h

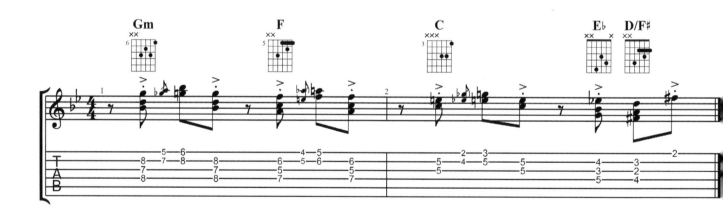

Chapter Six – Back Street Vamp Soloing Approach

If we view the harmony for *Back Street Vamp* as having an overall "G minor" tonal center, the progression can be seen as fusing together chords from different harmonized G minor scales. As you can hear, the point of the chord sequence is to gravitate *away* from G minor, then descend back *towards* it.

The Gm7, F7 and Ebmaj7 chords are all found in the harmonized G Natural Minor scale, but the C/E and D7 chords are a problem – they are both minor 7 chords in G Natural Minor. The C/E chord could be viewed as belonging to G Dorian (strictly speaking a C7) and the D7 to G Harmonic Minor.

So, this is a blues with a twist! This tune isn't rooted in any specific geographical location, but you can hear it has that cool, sophisticated urban feel.

When it comes to soloing over these changes, we can use the G Natural Minor scale (or its major relative Bb Major), for most of the tune, but we must take care to accommodate the major 3rd in the C/E chord. It also makes sense to treat the D7 as an altered dominant chord and use ideas from the G Harmonic Minor scale at this point in the tune.

With this in mind, let's explore some soloing ideas over this moody, atmospheric vamp.

In this first solo I begin with a phrase drawn from the G Natural Minor scale (G, A, Bb, C, D, Eb, F). As the progression begins again, I leave plenty of space and highlight the changes with small chord structures.

When we approach the C/E in bar six, this chord is anticipated from the end of bar five. Here I am still using G Natural Minor, but I've made sure to modify the scale so that I play an E natural rather than an Eb note.

At the end of bar six, over the D7 chord, I could have used the G Harmonic Minor scale to accommodate that chord but chose instead to stick with the natural minor scale. Superimposing G Natural Minor over D7 implies certain altered tension notes. In this phrase, the F note implies the #9 of D7 (enharmonically E#), the Eb the b9, and the Bb the #5 (enharmonically A#).

For the rest of the solo, notice that whenever the C/E chord occurs, I make sure to include an E note in my phrase.

Let me draw your attention to one final idea in this solo. In the second half of bar eight, I play a simple four-note phrase that outlines the Ebmaj7 chord. The notes are D (7th), Eb (root), D an octave higher, and C (6th). I then repeat this phrase, modifying it slightly by adding two notes, over the D7 chord. It's a common blues idea to play a phrase and repeat it up an octave, but the same phrase played over a different chord will highlight different chord tones or altered tensions. Over D7, the phrase implies the #5, b9 and 11th.

Example 6a

If you are the main harmonic instrument in your band as well as the soloist, you can take more liberties with the harmony than you could if you were playing with another guitarist or keyboard player. Since we are playing over a backing track of just bass and drums, we are free to spice up the chords and add extended or altered notes. This is the approach I take in bar two of this eight-bar solo. Once you've got your fingers around the chord shapes, be sure to punch them out and refer to the audio to nail the irregularly placed accents.

Example 6b

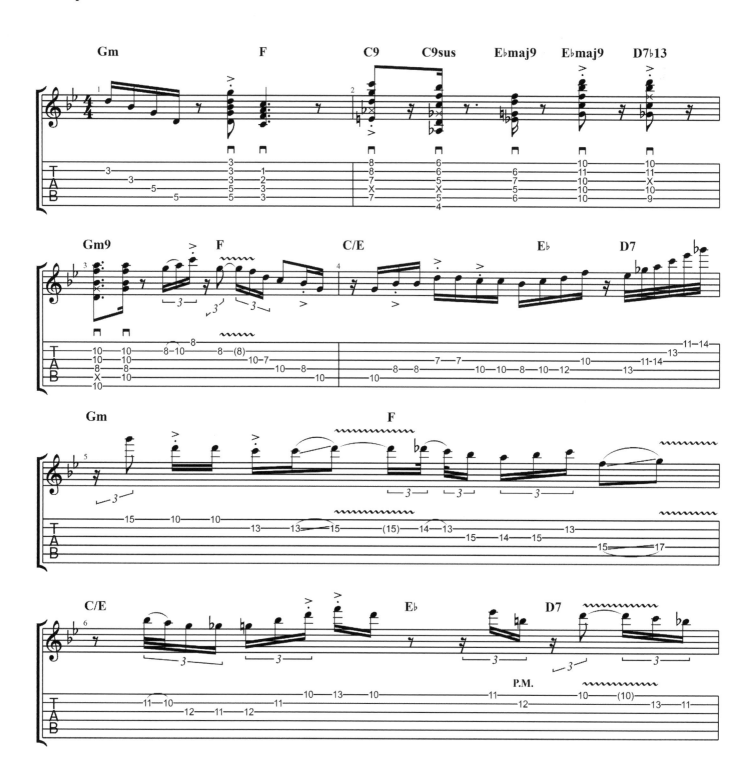

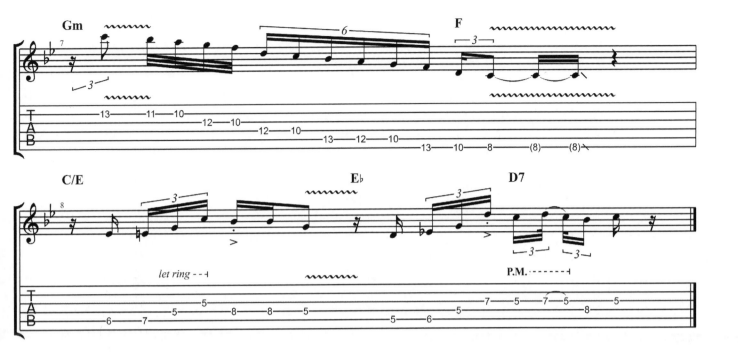

In this take on the solo, in bars 1-4 I outline the harmony by playing a double-stop idea. To create these lines, I'm using the notes of the G Natural Minor scale arranged as two-note structures, to create a stripped-down chordal motif.

G Natural Minor scale = G, A, Bb, C, D, Eb, F

A great way to get this idea into your playing is to visualize the scale mapped across the fretboard, then pick out two-note clusters that sit close together.

The diagram on the left below shows all the notes of the G Natural Minor scale in a seven-fret zone. The diagram on the right shows only the notes I used to create the phrase in bar one. Spend some time experimenting with this scale map and come up with your own double-stop phrases using notes on adjacent strings. (NB: I adapt this idea in bar two to accommodate the C major and D7 chords).

G Natural Minor Scale   Double-Stop Notes

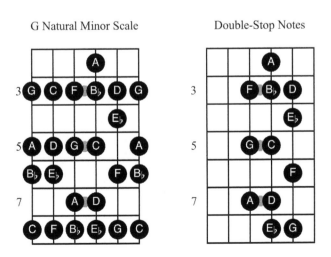

Notice the line I play over the transition from D7 back to G minor in bars 4-5. Over the D7 chord the notes are all from the G Harmonic Minor scale (G, A, Bb, C, D, Eb, F#) apart from one small passing note inflection. D7 is chord V in the harmonized G Harmonic Minor scale.

Over the G minor chord, I opted to use the G Dorian scale with one additional passing note. This scale has the notes G, A, Bb, C, D, E, F. Notice that it contains an E note, while the natural and harmonic minor scales have an Eb. This note gives the Dorian scale its distinctive sound. When played over a G minor chord, it implies a Gm6 sound.

I chose to close out this solo with some more colorful chord stabs. Give it a go!

Example 6c

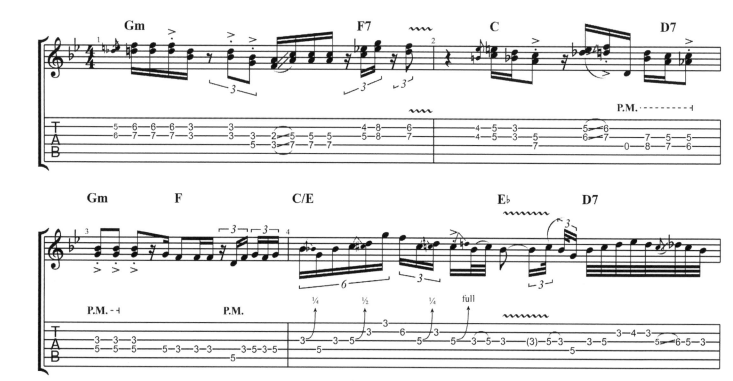

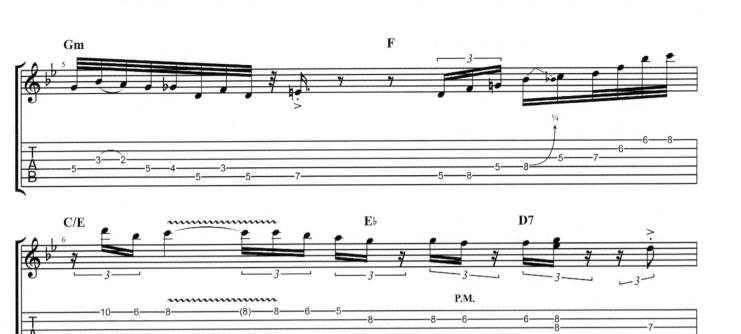

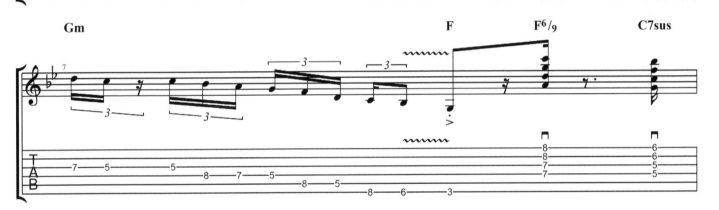

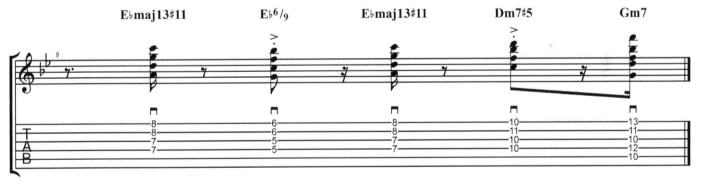

Chapter Seven – King Snake Rhythm Parts

In this chapter we're looking at a tune called *King Snake,* which is a back-to-basics, four-on-the-floor straight up 12-bar blues! Written in the key of E Major, this is the kind of tune you'll come across at blues jam sessions and is typical of the tunes we all endlessly jammed over when we were starting out. E Major is one of the most popular keys for guitar blues, as it allows beginner players to use open chords throughout – plus you can easily play low and high solos using standard pentatonic box shapes.

Here we will look at some ideas to spice up what could potentially be a very repetitive rhythm part, but first let's nail the rhythm in its basic form. The first four bars are based around an open position E minor chord (though you'll notice I may occasionally play an E Major). This part is all about the feel, so it's important to capture the groove and make sure you're really playing in the pocket.

First, listen to the audio for Example 7a. The audio demonstrates the full 12-bar pattern, but below I will comment on each four-bar section.

Palm muting with the strumming hand is the critical factor in getting this entire rhythm part to sound sharp but is especially important during bars 1-4. When using open chords for a part like this, it's important to keep them under control and prevent any open strings we don't want to hear from ringing out.

Keep your strumming loose and relaxed and allow your palm to float above the strings close to the bridge pickup. Apply light pressure with your palm to mute the strings when indicated by the "X" symbol. I always tell students to keep their strumming hand moving with a constant up/down rhythm, so it acts like a metronome. Then it's easier to use palm mutes to control which accents you want to pop out. This was pointed out to me a long time ago, and it sounds kind of obvious, but keep your strumming hand going – it will help you to find the right feel and groove.

The E minor chord alternates with an inversion of A Major (E, A, C#) at the second fret, and an inversion of G (D, G, B) using the open strings. The result is a familiar riff, made famous in tunes like David Bowie's *The Jean Genie.* Try it out now.

Example 7a

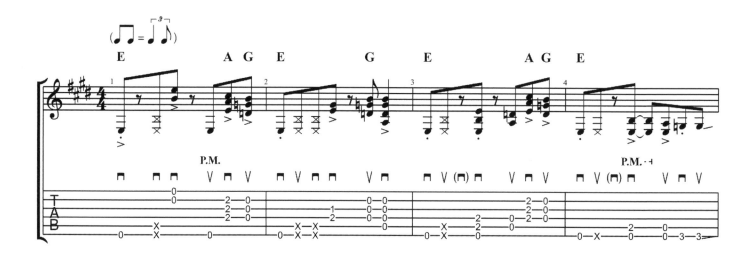

In bars 5-6, rather than use an open A chord we move to a barre chord instead, before returning to the main riff.

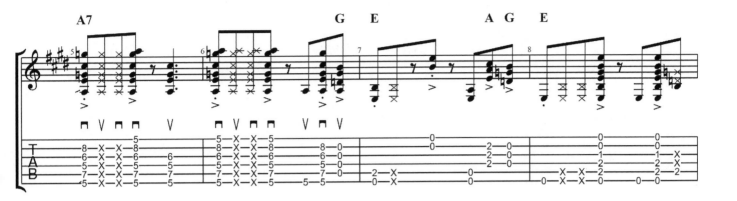

For the B7 to A7 chord change, I use simple three-note voicings.

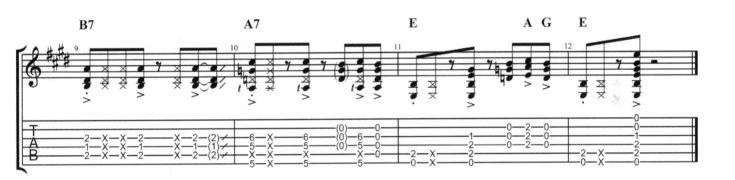

Now that you have the complete rhythm part in its basic form, play through it a few times using the backing track that accompanies this chapter. The chord shapes used are simple, so focus your attention on really making the rhythm groove.

Now let's look at some ideas for deviating from the main riff to keep things interesting. Example 7b introduces an idea that puts a nice twist on the harmony.

In bar one, the original chord is E minor, and my thought process was to borrow a chord from the relative major key of G Major. The notes on the D to B strings form a G major triad (G, B, D). If I play that while the bass player is holding down an E bass note, the result is the sound of an Em7 chord, but it creates interest because we are not used to hearing that D note on top of an E minor voicing.

If, at this point I'm thinking G Major, and I want to get back to E minor, then I need a connecting chord. What sounded good to my ears was an F# minor chord. This is chord ii in the key of E Major (remember the minor/major interchangeability of the blues) and it wants to resolve back to E. Although I'm thinking F# minor and playing an F#m11 voicing here, the bass player is still on E, so the overall effect is that of an E suspended chord.

In bar five, I continue to play the exact same shape, but the bass player is now playing an A root note. Superimposed over A, my G triad now suggests the sound of an A9 suspended chord. In bar six, the F#m11 shape I used in bar two, over an A bass note, implies A6 suspended. It's always worth experimenting with chord voicings over alternative root notes to see what different flavors you can bring out.

In bar nine, I play a B7#9 chord instead of a straight B7. Played here in second position, you can add a slight bend to the top note to make it sound more bluesy. This is followed by a different inversion of A7 to lead back into the main riff.

Example 7b

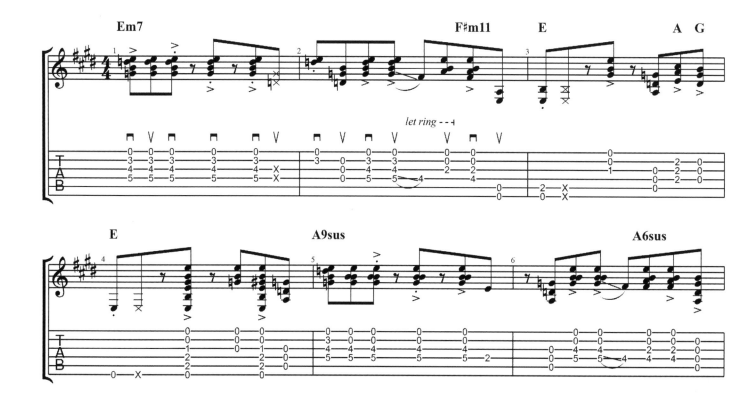

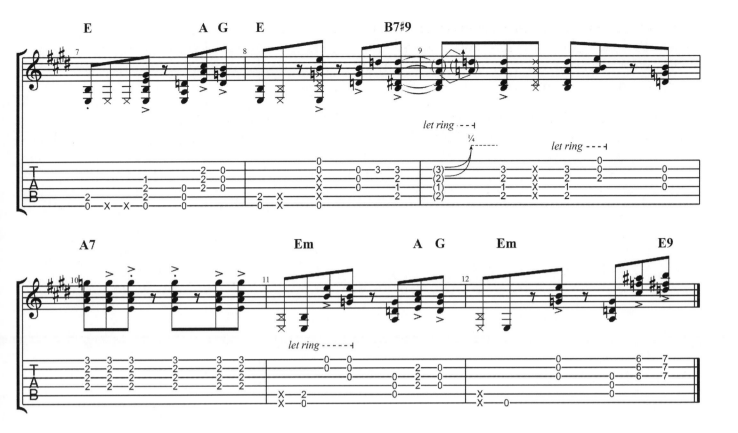

This alternative take on the rhythm part introduces a new tension in the first four bars. In bar one, I opt to play an E dominant chord, rather than E major or minor. We noted earlier that in a simple three chord blues, the lines are blurred between major and minor tonalities, but equally all three chords can be played as dominant 7 chords too.

Throughout bars 1-4, I change up the rhythm and play constant 1/8th note triplets. This "three over four" feel can be dramatic and effective as long as it's used sparingly. It's easy for the timing to become loose when playing triplets for several bars, so make sure you keep it tight.

In bar two, you can clearly hear that the harmony moves down a half step, and this creates tension over the E bassline, but what is happening here? To understand this idea, it might help you to play this sequence of chords:

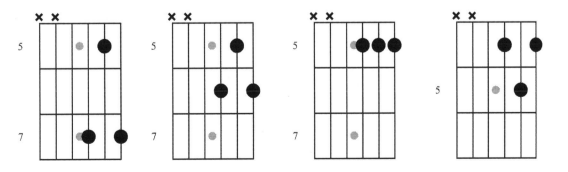

Each chord is a variation of E and the main idea at work is the chromatic descent on the high E string. In order, these shapes are E7, E6b5, Esusb6 and E major. I only use the first two shapes below, but from the sequence above, you can hear the direction of this idea and how it resolves. It's a movement that has been used in many blues and Rock 'n' Roll tunes.

Another twist in this take is the use of 9sus4 chords in bars 9-10. Below, B9sus4 is illustrated. Just move it down a whole step to play A9sus4. It's possible to play the bass note (indicated by a hollow circle) with your thumb over the neck, but you can also just leave that note to the bass player! The 9sus4 chord has such an open sound that it brings a completely different, modern flavor to the piece.

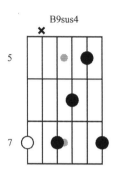

Example 7c

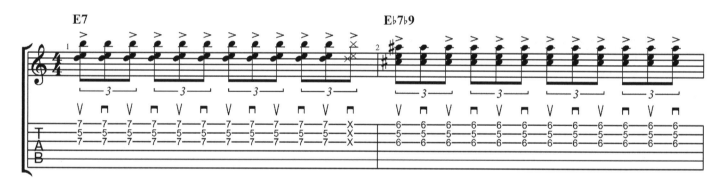

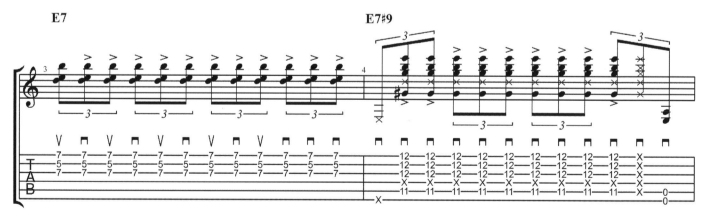

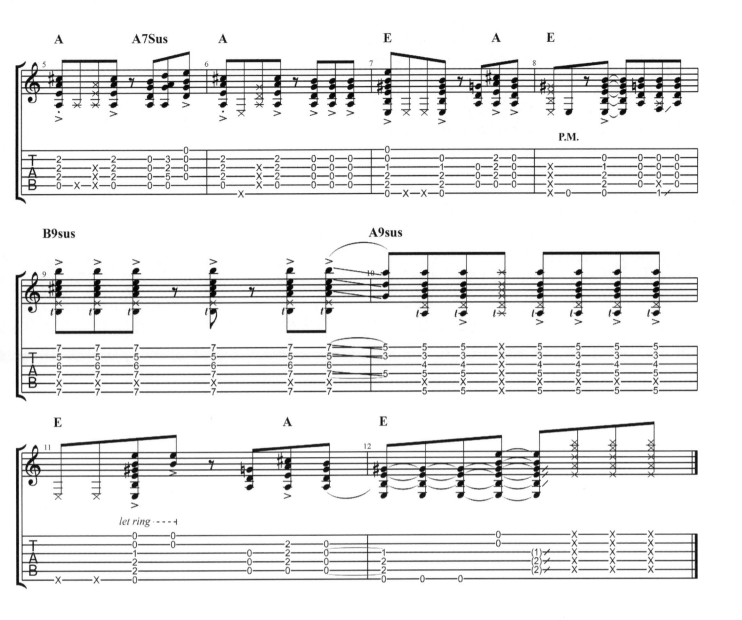

Let's introduce one more idea that will add variety to the rhythm part. This time, I focus on an E minor feel and again use the idea of *repurposing* chords i.e. using the same voicings over different bass notes.

In jazz/fusion, when playing over multiple bars of a minor chord, a common idea is to move the chord up by a half step or whole step, then return to the original chord to create tension and resolution. Here I use a *whole step* movement to create a riff. This movement is notated as Em7 to F#m7, and you can view it as moving briefly to the ii chord of E Major then back to E minor.

In bars 5-6, I use the exact same chord shapes while the bass player is holding down the A root note. As in Example 7b, the effect of superimposing Em7 over an A bass note is an A9 suspended sound. When we shift the voicing up a whole step, the F#m7 shape now sounds like an A6.

In bar nine, I hang onto the F#m7 chord shape, but now the bassist is holding down a B note, and this creates a B9sus4 sound. In the first half of bar ten, I'm still playing F#m7, though I've altered the shape slightly, and it creates the A6 sound again. In the second half of the bar, I move that shape down a whole step to make the A9sus4 sound again.

This is a lot to take in, but the main idea to take away here is to move chord voicings around the fretboard and see how they sound over different bass notes. Find the sounds that appeal to you – you can figure out why they work later!

As we return to the original riff in bars 11-12, we can hear how far we had gravitated away from it. Dropping back into this groove now provides some real contrast.

Example 7d

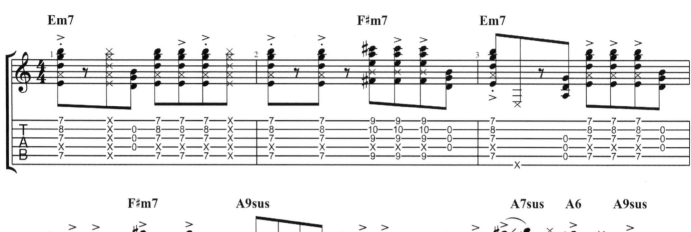

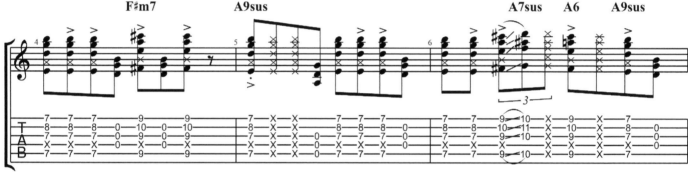

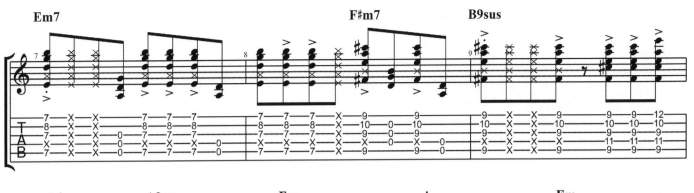

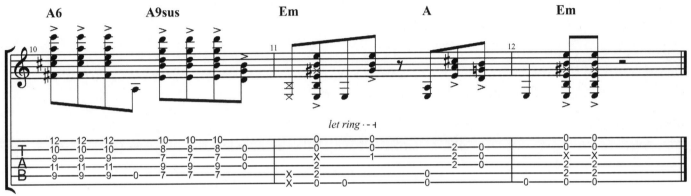

Next, it's time to look at some soloing ideas for *King Snake*.

Chapter Eight – King Snake Soloing Approach

For a tune named *King Snake* that has a strong, driving groove, it felt like a direct, aggressive approach was required for the solo. This tune is more in the Texas blues style and for the solo, I'm on the bridge pickup of my guitar throughout, driving the amp hard, and allowing the tone to naturally overdrive, not using too much distortion. For this solo, I really wanted the licks to cut through.

In this first solo take, I play an opening lick, then repeat it right away. The idea here is *phrase displacement*. The first time I play the ascending run as a pickup bar and hit the high E note on beat 1. The second time, I begin the run on beat 2 of bar two. This time I also include a slight pause before hitting the high E, which further breaks up the lick rhythmically.

If you learn a cool lick, make sure you don't always play it in the same place in a piece of music. You might always play your favorite lick starting on a downbeat or always on an offbeat, for instance. Displacing a lick is like having a new lick, because it will sound fresh in a different context.

Contrast is important when taking a solo. If you're going to play a fast lick, contrasting it with something slow will make it sound more dramatic. For example, in bars 4-5 I play some slower, expressive bends that set up the quick burst in bar six. This run is based around the E Blues scale box position at the twelfth fret. The Bb note (notated A# here) on the G string, fret 15, when played over an A7 chord, fleetingly suggests an A7b9 sound.

There is another example of contrast in the final five bars of the solo. Contrast doesn't have to be fast versus slow, it can be loud versus quiet, or motif licks versus runs. In bars 8-9 I pull things back slightly with palm muted double stops, and in bar ten I build up to the final fast run. After the run, I deliberately leave quite a lot of space before I begin a second pass.

Try playing the final lick in bar eleven all legato. Your preference might be to pick everything, but I find that using pull-offs for this kind of lick makes it sound smoother. For the fast triplet beginning on beat 1, fret the A note on the D string, fret 7 with your third finger, then either quickly slide to fret 8 and back again (like me) or use your pinkie to play fret 8.

Example 8a

This next take on the solo is all about making the most of bends. Bending notes is a huge part of the language of the blues, but bending a note can sound sterile if you don't inject it with some emotion. Here are three ideas you can use to make your bends sound more soulful.

First, if you're going to bend a note, have a clear destination in mind and make sure you reach it. Beginner guitar players will often bend a note imprecisely and the result is, it's not clear what note they are aiming for. In blues there are several types of bend players will use: a half step, a whole step, a curl (a 1/4 bend that just hints at another note), or a wide bend (more than a whole step). It's a good idea to practice each of these bends so that you can hit the note you want with clarity. I also recommend that you hold your bent target note in pitch before adding any vibrato.

Second, in the blues you can take your time bending into the target note. Taking some time to reach your destination will grab your audience's attention as you move from an outside sounding note to an inside sounding one. Listen to how I do this in bars 1-4. My idea here was to keep aiming for a higher target note and the bends are not rushed.

Third, you can use a wide vibrato while controlling a bend, so that you move through more than one target note. Check out bar six of the solo. It's impossible to convey this in notation, so you'll need to listen to the audio for Example 8b. I begin with a whole step bend on the G string, fret 14, then slowly release the bend while applying a wide vibrato – almost shaking the neck of the guitar. As the bend is released, it moves from a whole step to a half step bend, before returning to the original note.

In bar ten of this solo, I chose to highlight the sound of the A7 chord, rather than playing an E Blues scale type lick. Split into triplet phrases, this line contains all the notes of an A7 chord (A, C#, E, G) but also B and D notes, respectively the 9th and 11th.

Now have a go at the solo and make sure to wring every bit of emotion you can out of those bends!

Example 8b

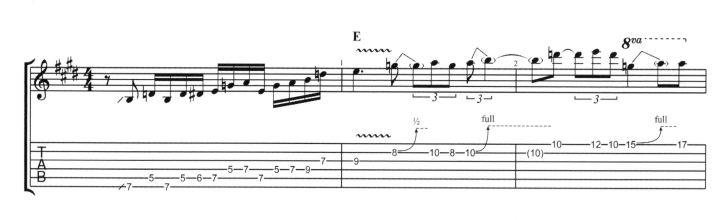

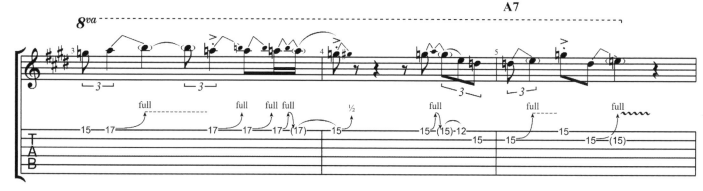

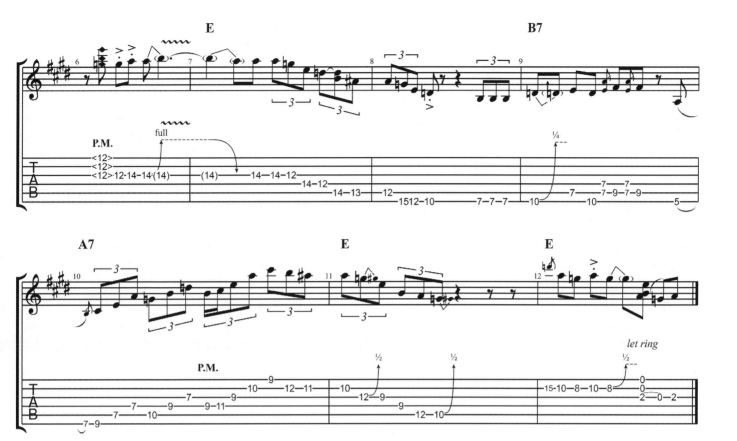

In the next solo, I make the most of the fact that we are playing in the key of E and use the lower register to play riff-like phrases. This is the kind of idea Jimi Hendrix would often use, utilizing open strings where possible and playing double-stops or chord fragments. This approach blurs the line between what is lead and what is rhythm playing.

Play the riffs in bars 1-7 with some real attitude and don't worry too much about the timing. It's meant to feel loose, slightly behind the beat, and you can let strings ring out. It doesn't need to sound too clean.

In the last two bars, play the repeating bend with a hard pick attack. It needs to sound "urgent" as it cuts across the beat. Pick every note of the final bend.

Example 8c

The final solo builds on the idea that began at the end of the previous solo. The opening statement in bars 1-2 is a type of question and answer phrase, but only uses two notes. It uses fast slides for effect and shows that you don't have to do something very technical in order to grab the audience's attention. People relate much more to your passion.

Simplicity and repetition have always been the backbone of the blues, and in bars 3-4 we have a repeating bend that cuts across the beat to create a three-over-four feel. The phrase spills over into the first half of bar five.

Bar six has another example of how you can access more than one pitch with a bend. Played over the A7 chord, the half step bend on the B string, fret 13, alternates between C and C#. It could easily have been picked, but the bend sounds more expressive. The target C# note is the 3rd of A7. This short riff concludes with the 5th (E) and b7 (G).

A final question and answer phrase spans bars 8-10 as we begin to bring the solo down, indicating that it's coming to a conclusion, and bars 11-12 give it a definite ending.

Be sure to jam out all of these ideas over the provided backing track.

Example 8d

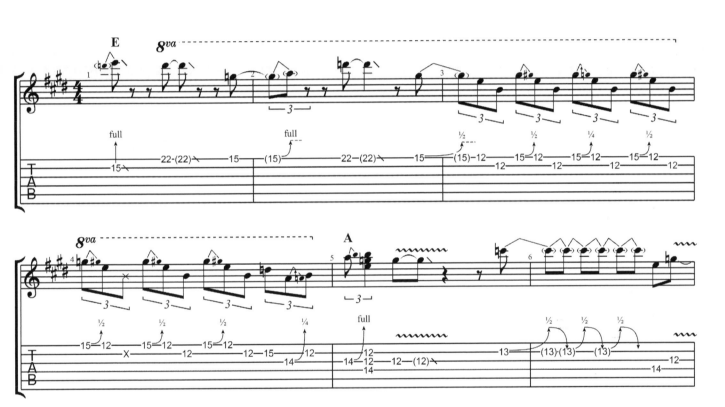

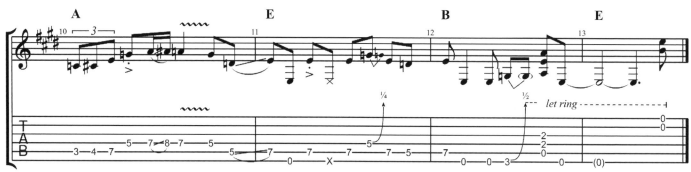

Chapter Nine – Roll With It Rhythm Parts

Roll With It is a classic one-chord vamp in A. It's a traditional *boogie* – the term used to describe a repetitive swung note or shuffle rhythm. The "boogie" name comes from *boogie-woogie*, a genre of blues that was popular in the 1920s, normally played on piano.

This is the kind of groove-based idea that crops up all the time in jam sessions. A one-chord vamp means it's easy for anyone to participate, since there is no chord progression to deal with, but this brings its own challenge: *how do we keep things interesting?* It's easy to run out of ideas very quickly when soloing over one chord, so it's good to have some strategies up your sleeve for keeping things fresh.

In *Roll With It*, the bass plays a very traditional line with an ascending figure, while the guitar plays a complementary part that descends, so there is some contrary motion between the parts. The riff is based around a simple open A5 chord in second position.

Hold down the A5 chord throughout the riff, barring it with the first finger. Without moving the first finger, use the second finger to play the G note on the low E string and the C note on the A string. This rhythm needs to be played with a lot of attack and attitude but be careful to avoid the B string when strumming. If you catch it when playing the A5 chord it's no problem but it'll produce a horrible clash over the C6 chord.

Have a listen to the audio then play through the riff. Practice to the backing track and keep rolling it around until you get it sounding nice and smooth and it's grooving.

Example 9a

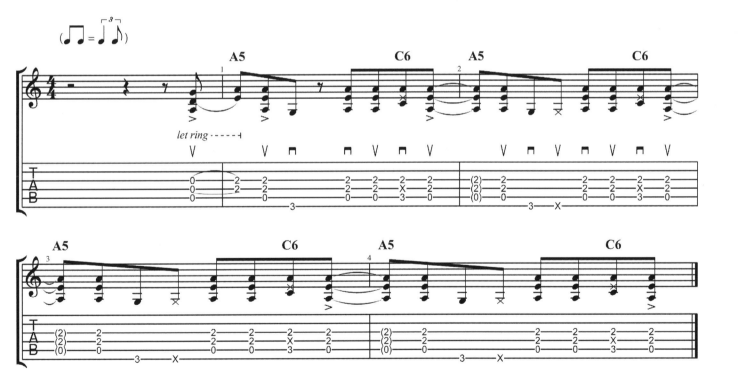

As with all blues, we can give this tune a major or minor emphasis. A more modern approach to comping over this vamp is to use A minor as the focal point and combine it with a stripped-back D chord voicing to create a rhythmic riff. This immediately gives the piece a lot more attack and energy and, of course, it creates a completely different kind of vibe.

Example 9b

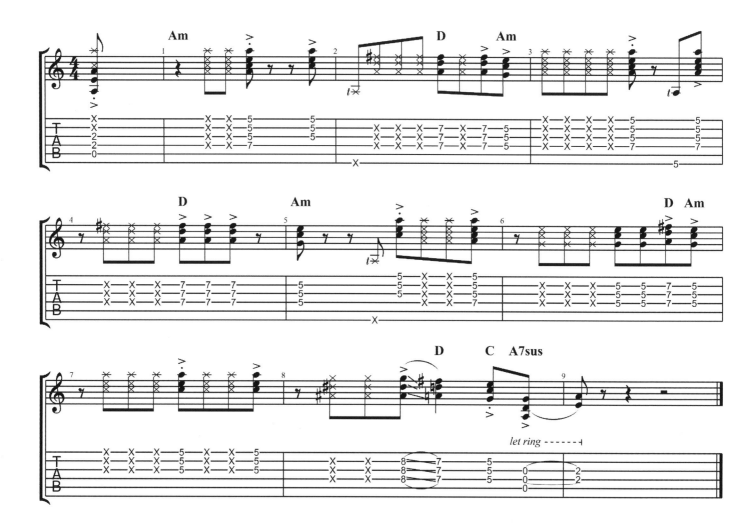

When playing over a one-chord vamp, especially where the bass is playing a simple repeating pattern, we can take more liberties with our chordal ideas. We can switch between major and minor ideas, but we can also make the main chord a dominant 7. In the next example you'll hear that this gives the piece a brighter sounding, uplifting feel. Here I use a three-note A7 voicing that has the root, 5th and b7 but no 3rd. I use partial E minor and D major voicings as passing chords, then return to A minor rather than A7. The E minor is optional and second time around I omit it. Go with what your ears prefer!

Example 9c

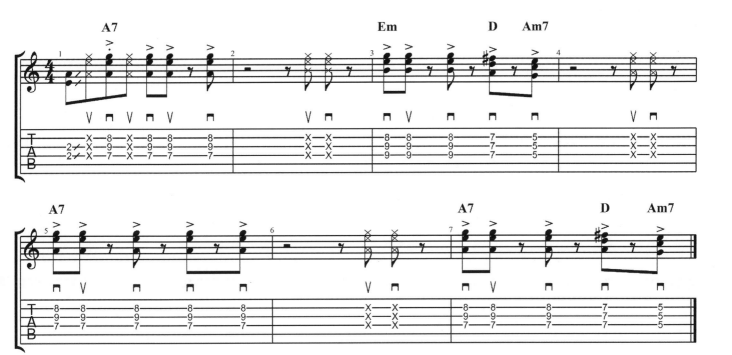

We noted earlier that a common idea in jazz when comping over a static minor chord is to modulate back and forth by a whole step. Here's a comping idea that moves between A minor and B minor. You can also use their relative major chords here – i.e. C in place of A minor and D in place of B minor – and freely switch between them. When playing this idea, strum quite freely and aim to give it a real swing. Check out the audio to capture my feel.

Example 9d

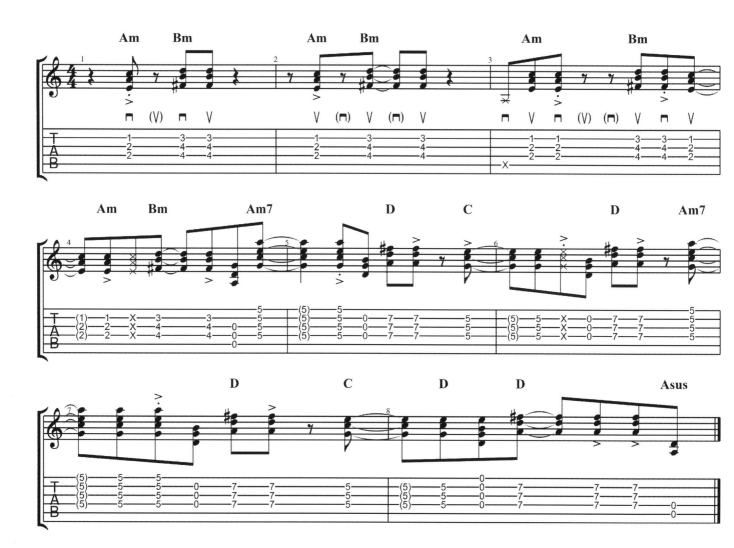

For an even more modern take on the one-chord vamp, try this example that uses an Am9 chord as the focal point. The idea here is to approach the Am9 chromatically from below and above. It gives the piece an *inside-outside* feel that is very different from the riff we began with. Experiment with this idea over the backing track and try altering the rhythms to suit your taste.

Example 9e

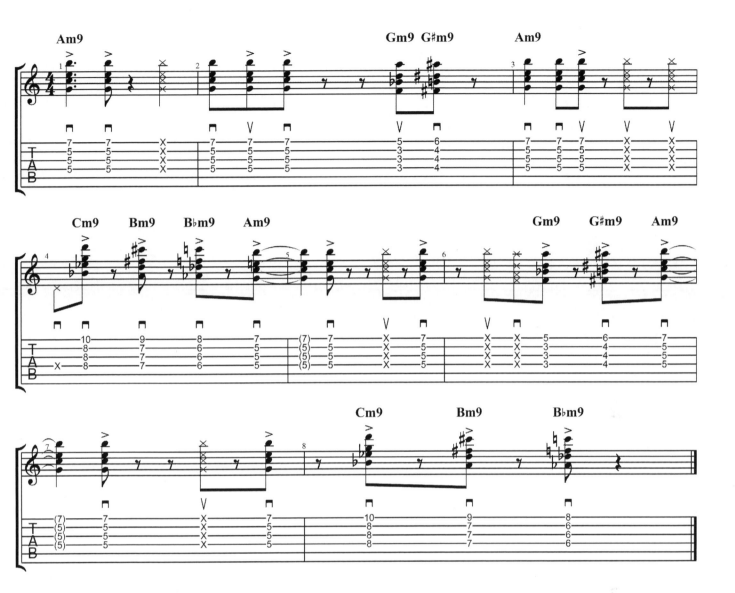

Here is one final comping idea, based on Example 9d, that moves between A minor and B minor. This time we are using higher voicings and chord stabs, rather than strumming.

Example 9f

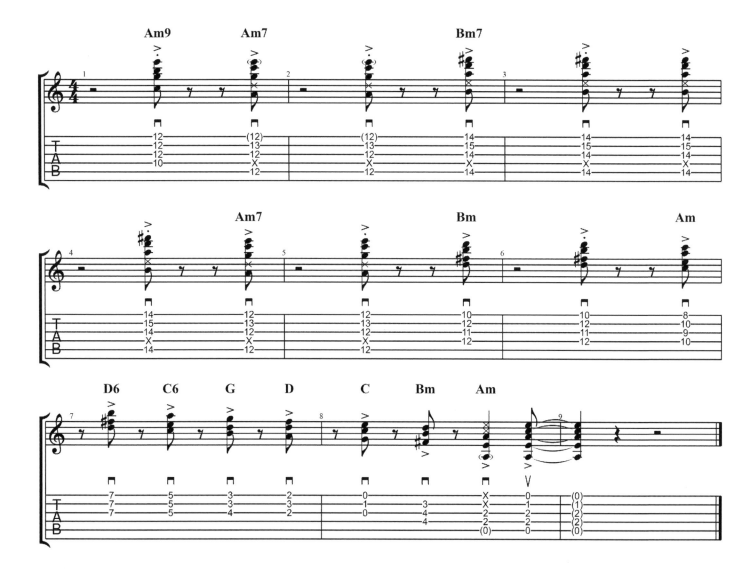

Chapter Ten – Roll With It Soloing Approach

Since *Roll With It* is a straight-ahead boogie tune, for the most part, I take a straight-ahead approach to soloing over it. What's needed here is plenty of attitude!

However, this first solo highlights an idea I like to use that fuses together two scales. Over an A vamp, the A Blues scale is an obvious choice.

A Blues scale = A, C, D, Eb, E, G

It contains the useful b5 tension note (Eb) that can be used so effectively in blues licks and runs.

But I also like to use the A Natural Minor scale:

A Natural Minor = A, B, C, D, E, F, G

This scale doesn't have the b5 note of the Blues scale, but it adds a B note, which over an A7 chord implies the sound of A9, and also an F note, which implies A7#5.

Rather than think about two separate scales, we can merge the two and think in terms of a hybrid scale. In fifth position, the hybrid pattern looks like this:

Hybrid Natural Minor/
Blues Scale

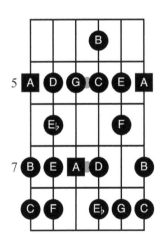

This approach allows us to play standard bluesy vocabulary, but easily add color and tension when we want to. I don't use the #5 tension in the following solo, but you'll hear me reference the 9th, such as on the bend in bar six where I bend from the note A to B on the B string. When it's surrounded by lots of straight ahead blues licks, emphasizing the 9th brings a different flavor.

Example 10a

Just as we might switch between major and minor chord voicings in the blues, it's very common to switch between major and minor scales. This lick begins with an A Major Pentatonic idea but by bar four has morphed into the A Minor Blues scale.

In bars 10-13 there is a repeating bend idea that moves from an E to A note. It could be a major or minor lick – both notes belong to the A major/minor pentatonic scales. Make sure you extend the bend by the full amount each time and pay attention to the change in rhythm as the lick speeds up.

Example 10b

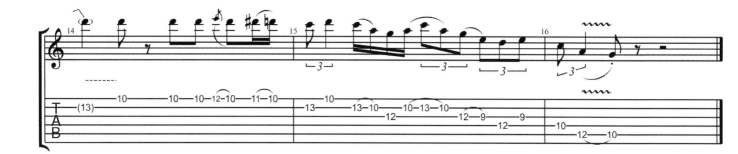

Here is a shorter idea for you. This kind of lick is ideal if you are playing with just bass and drums and you want to create a big sound. It's an aggressive double-stop string bend idea that cuts across the beat. Here you'll bend the B and G strings a half step simultaneously from the seventh fret. The way I play this is to lightly rest my first finger on fret 5 and push the bend up with my third and pinkie fingers, using the second finger for support. If you are using heavier strings, you may need to use the power of the second and third fingers to execute the bend.

Example 10c

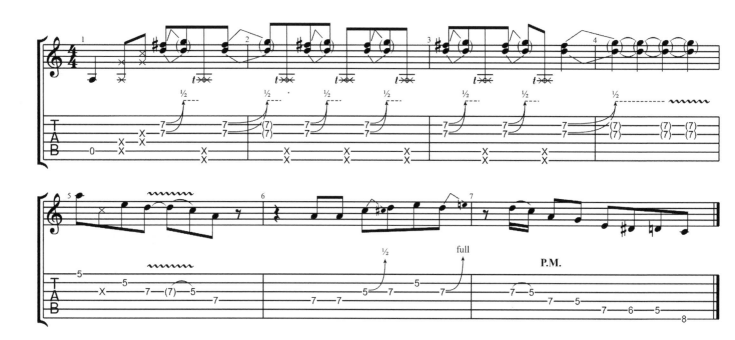

This take on the solo provides contrast by combining some single note phrases with a riff-like idea. In bars 1-3, get the most out of those two notes by playing with plenty of pick attack and applying a fast, wide vibrato to the C note on the high E string.

In the latter half of the solo I play a riff idea that morphs into a chromatic pattern. Again, I wanted to play with the rhythm here, so the lick speeds up and the 1/8th note triplet passage gives us that "three-over-four" feel we've used in previous ideas.

Example 10d

Chapter Eleven – Sam's Jam Rhythm Parts

The final tune we're going to look at is called *Sam's Jam,* which is a different kind of blues for you to explore. It's a tribute to Magic Sam, the great Chicago bluesman, who learned to play by studying the records of Muddy Waters and Little Walter. He settled in Chicago aged 19 and his guitar playing earned him lots of gigs and a record deal after only a year in town. To me, he is one of the unsung heroes of urban blues and deserves much wider recognition. He is less well known because he died very young, aged just 32. But, for those familiar with his music, he is celebrated for his unique sound, which set him apart from his contemporaries.

This is a *surf beat* tune that will give you the opportunity to jam on a funky blues groove. Surf music goes back to Southern California of the late 1950s and is usually in straight 4/4 time, almost never a shuffle. It has a bright, upbeat, driving feel that propels the music forward.

In *Sam's Jam*, the drums remain very straight throughout, while the bass plays a grooving, syncopated line. This is the perfect backing for playing some funkier blues guitar.

Example 11a sets out the basic rhythm part for this tune.

Sam's Jam is in the key of G minor and the rhythm is based around a G minor riff. The notes on the B and high E strings are G Natural Minor scale notes arranged in fourths and these "bounce" off a C major triad inversion at the fifth fret.

To get this part sound crisp and funky it's important to mute any unplayed strings well. My approach is to get the fretting hand to do all the hard work. Lightly hold down a G minor chord in third position, omitting the bass note. Play both notes on the bottom two strings with the pinkie finger and allow your hand to move backwards and forwards slightly, alternating between third and fourth position. Holding the chord shape but only plucking the required strings will mute the unplayed string sufficiently and allow you to strum freely with the picking hand.

In bar five, we need to make a small adjustment to the riff to accommodate the C7 chord, but the overall sound of the riff is still there. Give it a try.

Example 11a

Next, here are some alternative ways to approach the rhythm part. This version retains the funkiness but has a slightly more driving feel. For contrast, in bar two we move to a rootless Gm7 voicing. In bar five, the standard C7 becomes a C9 chord. In bars 7-8 I improvised a riff based around the simple G minor shape. You can experiment with this idea to create a variety of chordal "fills", especially on this kind of funky groove. In this version I play smaller versions of the D7 and C7 chords, voiced with the 5th on the bottom to produce a fatter sound, before returning to the original riff at the end.

Example 11b

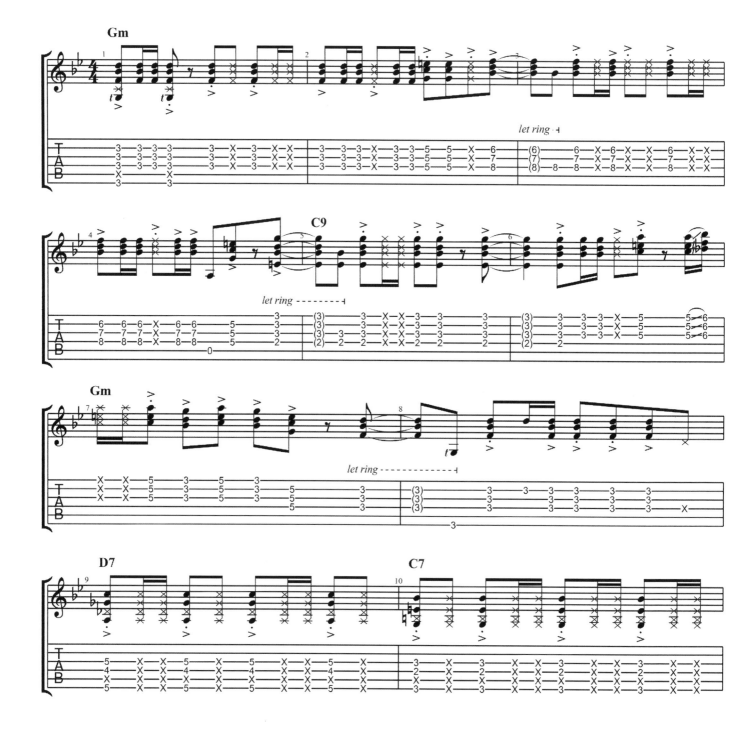

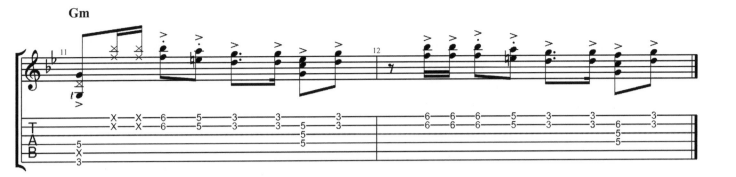

An easy way to push the energy up another notch is to play higher voicings of the chords. You'll be familiar with the Gm7 shape in tenth position here. In bar five I play a three-note voicing of C6, then move this shape down a whole step. Because the bass player is holding down a C note in the bass at this point, the chord shape implies a C9 sound. Using higher voicings for the D7 and C7 chords rounds off this take.

Example 11c

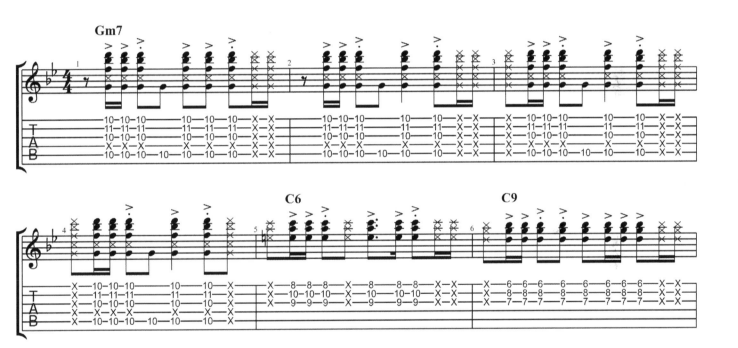

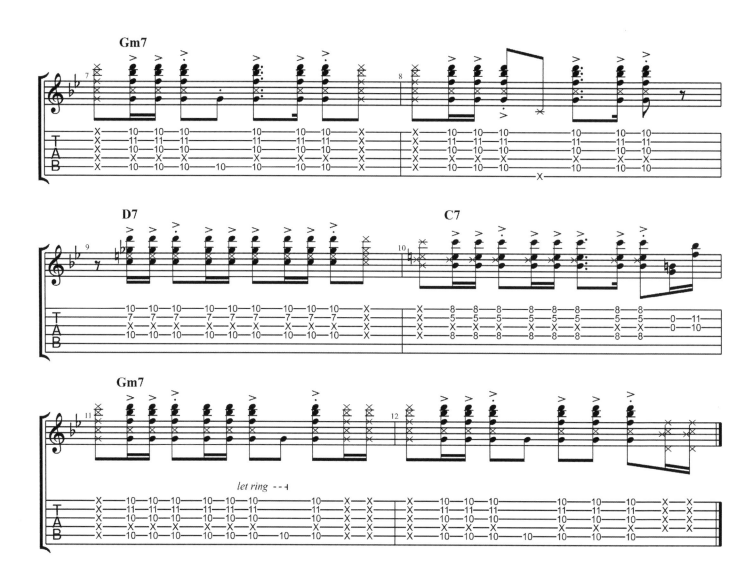

Here is one more approach for you. To create a different mood, here I'm using an unusual voicing for the G minor chord. It's a Gm11 that utilizes the open D string. From low to high the voicing is arranged 5th, b3, 11th and b7. The result is a jangly chord that creates a spacious, open sound.

Play the Gm11 by holding down the high E and B string notes with the first finger and fretting the G string note with the pinkie. Bring the third finger over the top to fret the bass note on the low E string, fret 3. Using this grip for the chord makes the change to C7 easier.

We also have a more colorful version of the V chord in this version. In place of a standard D7, we have D7sus4. The voicing used here might not be your go-to version (it's more normally played as a fifth position barre chord), but this way maintains the jangly chord feel.

Example 11d

Chapter Twelve – Sam's Jam Soloing Approach

In an earlier chapter, we briefly touched on the concept of *vocal phrasing*. Many of my favorite musicians appeal to me because they have this skill in abundance. Players like B.B. King and jazz guitarist Jim Hall spring to mind. The alto saxophonist Paul Desmond was also a great influence on me in this regard (my first instrument was alto sax).

Vocal phrasing simply means to phrase your melodic lines in a way that emulates the human voice. Paul Desmond had an incredible facility to play beautiful, lyrical phrases. B.B. King's playing was always full of soul and charged with emotion. Jim Hall was one of the great storytellers of jazz guitar, whose improvisations were never random but took you on a journey. They had all learned the art of vocal phrasing.

If you have ever tried singing a melodic line before repeating it on guitar, you'll know that this method will often create more interesting and natural sounding melodic ideas. Of all musical styles, the blues is fertile ground for vocal phrasing. In the blues we have an emphasis on question and answer phrasing, but also expressive bends. Both are great tools for developing a vocal quality to your lines.

In this first solo take, you'll begin by playing a series of short phrases with bends. The notes come from the G Natural Minor scale. Notice that the phrase in bar two is identical to bar one, it's just been shifted up a minor third (three frets). These phrases pass quickly, but your goal is to get as much emotion as you can out of each one and aim for that vocal sound. Listen to the audio and you'll hear that I don't bend into the note too quickly and I apply lots of vibrato. The effect is hopefully to give the lines the quality of someone singing with emotion. Notice too that there is a clear breath between each phrase.

Example 12a

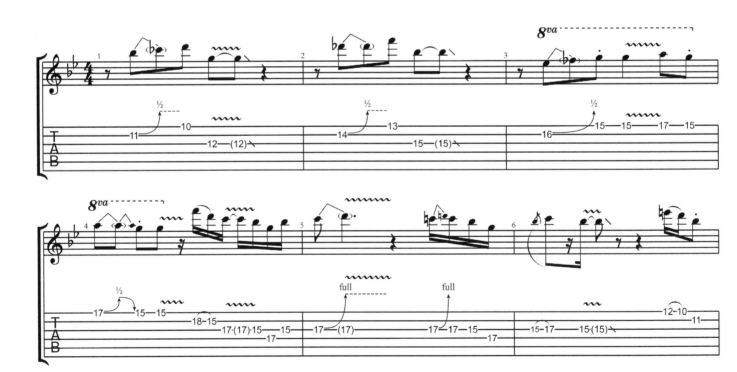

This take on the solo opens with a rhythmic repeating lick. All the notes come from the G Natural Minor scale. For the quick phrase on the high E string I'm picking every note, but you could play it with hammer-ons and pull-offs if you prefer.

Let me highlight the more complex lick that is played in bar three. Back in Chapter Ten we looked at how it's possible to create a useful hybrid minor scale by combining the notes of the natural minor and blues scales. I'm using the same idea here. All the notes come from the combined G Natural Minor and G Blues scales – except one (eagle-eyed readers will spot that I play one note on the open B string, technically the major 3rd rather than the minor 3rd).

Here is how the scale is laid out in third position. As before, jam over the backing track using this scale and see what licks you can come up with.

To learn the lick in bar three, slow things right down and view it as four interlocking phrases.

Hybrid Natural Minor/
Blues Scale

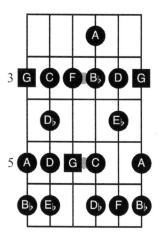

Example 12b

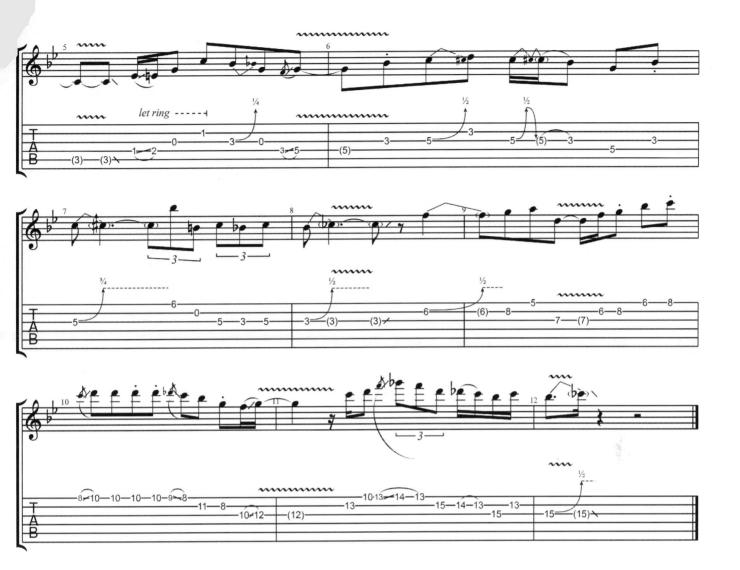

Here is a shorter idea that shows how you can take a simple motif and develop it by making very small changes. Again, here you should aim to get the most expression you can out of the bends, especially in bars 4-5. You goal is to achieve that vocal sound and pack the phrases with emotion.

Example 12c

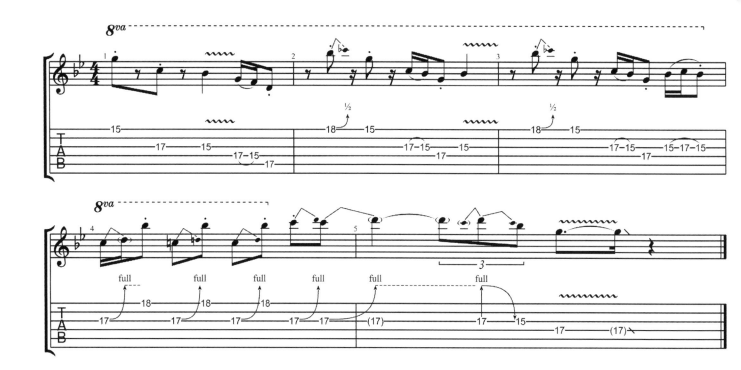

To conclude this chapter, here is a short double-stop idea you can use over a minor chord vamp. Here I am not thinking about scales, but more about how these two-note structures relate to a G minor chord.

The first two notes (D and F) are the 5th and b7 of G minor. The next two (C and E) imply the 11th and 6th. The next ones are the 3rd and 5th, and so on. If this feels like too much of a theory-heavy approach, you can just trust your ears and move these two-note shapes around the neck, listening to how they sound over the backing track. If something sounds good to you, then it is good! Have fun and don't be afraid to try things out.

Example 12d

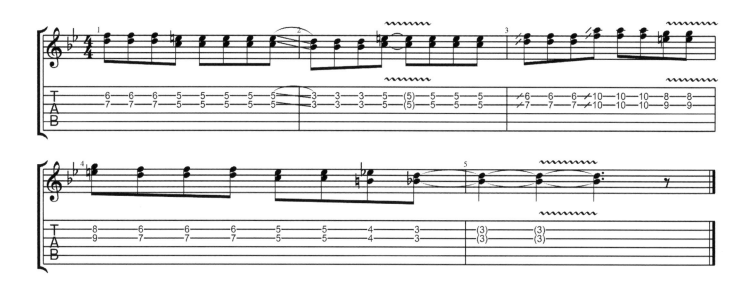

Conclusion

I hope you've enjoyed this journey through the Urban Blues. We've looked at the urban influences of Louisiana, Illinois, Texas and California, and also seen how Afro-Cuban grooves seeped into the Blues. Along the way, I trust you've learnt some useful rhythm approaches you can apply, plenty of blues soloing vocabulary, and an insight into how I think as a musician.

Take some time to go back over the licks you really enjoyed and play then in different zones of the fretboard, and in different keys. This is the best way to absorb them into your playing. Also, put your own twist on my ideas. Take a lick and adapt it, this way it will become personal to you, a part of *your* blues vocabulary.

You'll learn the most by jamming over the supplied backing tracks and simply experimenting with ideas. Take risks and try stuff out. Often, you'll have a happy accident and "discover" a new lick you really like. When this happens, play it lots of times and really embed it.

Have fun with your music and I'll see you on the road!

Robben

Made in United States
Orlando, FL
02 December 2021

11067141R00054